Borderline Personality Disorder Workbook

DBT Strategies and Exercises to Manage Symptoms and Improve Well-Being

Suzette Bray, LMFT

callisto
publishing
an imprint of Sourcebooks

Illustrations © marukopum/iStock
Author photo courtesy of Linda Bradley Photography
Art Directors: Lisa Forde and Lisa Schreiber
Art Producer: Casey Hollister
Editor: Adrian Potts
Production Editor: Ellina Litmanovich
Production Manager: Martin Worthington

Published by Callisto Publishing LLC C/O Sourcebooks LLC
P.O. Box 4410, Naperville, Illinois 60567-4410
(630) 961-3900
callistopublishing.com

Printed and bound in China
OGP 10 9 8 7 6 5 4 3 2 1

*As always, for my son Finn
and for my clients,
past, present, and future.*

Contents

Introduction

Hello there, reader! I am so glad you picked up this book. Whether you or someone you care about has been diagnosed with borderline personality disorder (BPD), or you suspect that diagnosis applies, you may have heard a lot of conflicting and alarming information. Perhaps you're relieved, thinking, "Finally, a name for what I'm dealing with." Or you might be worried or ashamed, because this diagnosis can carry some stigma with it. BPD can seem like bad news thanks to people, both health professionals and others, who don't know the good news about the excellent treatments and encouraging outcomes for folks dealing with this diagnosis. Because of my years of caring for folks with BPD, I am thrilled to share with you more accurate and hopeful information.

I'm proud to say that I have dedicated my career to helping those living with BPD. I have treated folks with this diagnosis for many years, and I'm intensively trained in dialectical behavior therapy (DBT), the gold-standard treatment for BPD. I owned and operated a comprehensive DBT program for many years. BPD is close to my heart. I have family members who have struggled with, and learned to manage and overcome, the symptoms of the diagnosis. And because being more emotionally sensitive than most is common among both those with BPD and the professionals who help them, I myself have benefited greatly from the skills that are taught in DBT treatment. I am truly grateful to have worked with those who moved from despairing to thriving because of the life-changing power of DBT. Their courage and hard work are awe-inspiring.

As you complete this workbook you'll learn lots of helpful information, skills, and tips for managing BPD symptoms and increasing your overall well-being. But, please remember, a workbook is no replacement for a trained, expert therapist or psychiatrist. If you are experiencing debilitating anxiety, depression, or urges to harm yourself, it is vital that you reach out for professional assistance. There is absolutely no shame in seeking help. I've provided resources for finding expert help in the Resources section (page 158).

Whatever your relationship to BPD, I'm confident this book will empower you to create lasting change. Learning new skills and ways of thinking is not always easy. But I'll be with you every step of the way, sharing resources that I've seen to be incredibly helpful. I am thrilled to offer my experience and my hope to you. And I applaud your courage and your willingness to take charge of your symptoms and move toward the life you want.

Let's get started!

—Suzette

How to Use This Book

This workbook is designed to help you better understand borderline personality disorder, examine your experiences with it, and learn practical skills to manage your symptoms.

In part 1 of the book, I'll guide you through an overview of borderline personality disorder and how it's treated. We'll start by reviewing how the BPD diagnosis evolved. We'll examine the stigma and controversy about the diagnosis, and see how Marsha Linehan reimagined the diagnosis and created dialectical behavior therapy. You'll see how others experience the symptoms of this diagnosis and learn that you are not alone.

Then, in chapter 2, we'll look more deeply at dialectical behavior therapy, DBT, an evidence-based treatment for BPD. You'll see how to set yourself up for success using the principles of this therapy, whether you're working with a therapist or on your own.

With that established, part 2 of the book will guide you into a deeper understanding of the key DBT skills you can use to help manage your symptoms and equip you with practical exercises to apply in your everyday life. Chapter 3 will introduce you to the practice of mindfulness, the core skill of DBT. In chapter 4, you'll learn about how to tolerate distress and get through bad situations without making them worse. Chapter 5 will bring you an understanding of difficult emotions and how to regulate them. Chapter 6 is all about improving your relationships through interpersonal effectiveness. And in chapter 7 we put it all together and set you up to keep honing and practicing the skills you have learned.

That sounds like a lot, doesn't it? Well, the good news is that you'll find many of the skills to be simple to use. You will likely encounter new concepts throughout the book, but if you focus on applying different skills as often as possible, you should start to notice a difference. Not immediately, but over time.

Many of the skills are simple, but successfully mastering and applying them can be challenging at times. Every chapter includes an affirmation that you can use to uplift and encourage yourself in continuing your practice. Always remember to be kind to yourself. Take a break from this book when you feel the need. Show yourself compassion and caring, and follow your intuition as to what you are ready to tackle.

And one especially important note: Self-harming behaviors and suicidal thoughts are common among people who are diagnosed with BPD. Don't take these issues lightly. Please seek professional help if you are in danger of harming yourself or others. If you are experiencing a life-threatening situation, please reach out for assistance. If you do not have immediate access to a professional who understands your situation and how to help you, the Suicide and Crisis Lifeline can be reached toll-free at 988. I have included more options in the Resources section (page 158).

Finally, while this workbook can be used on its own, you may also wish to pair it with the reflective writing prompts of the companion *Borderline Personality Disorder Journal*.

PART I

Understanding Borderline Personality Disorder

They say that knowledge is power, so in this first part of the book we're going to empower you with the facts about borderline personality disorder (BPD), its symptoms, its possible causes, and treatment options. You'll discover how dialectical behavior therapy (DBT), the most researched and documented treatment for BPD, can be extremely beneficial to individuals dealing with difficult emotions, behaviors, and relationships, which are the hallmarks of BPD. By the finish of these first two chapters, you'll be ready to dive into the strategies that will bring about healing.

CHAPTER 1

Let's Talk about BPD

We'll begin with diagnostic information about BPD; that is, how it's defined and some history about how the diagnosis evolved. And along the way, we'll spotlight the strength and courage of people who live with, manage, and overcome this diagnosis. You will learn about common misconceptions about this diagnosis, the stigma that results, and why that stigma is undeserved. And perhaps for the first time, you'll hear about the common experiences of people with BPD and how treatment can and does improve lives. In fact, let's start with that.

Sharon's Story: Figuring Things Out

Sharon always had been a big feeler. Her joy was heightened when someone was kind to her or when she witnessed humanity's generosity. A sunset would bring her great delight, but she would also feel grief because the experience was soon to end. In a similar way, Sharon was frightened of being abandoned by those she cared about. When she saw injustice, she felt anger that pushed her toward creating change. When she loved, she loved hard. And when she felt like someone was upset with her, Sharon could feel overwhelming shame and rage.

In some ways, Sharon's emotions were a great gift, fueling her activism, her creativity, and her love, care, and empathy for others. Other times, emotions felt like her worst enemy. It was not uncommon for Sharon to feel overwhelmed, numb, or empty when experiencing a negative emotion. Sometimes she would feel compelled to engage in risky behaviors, such as thinking about cutting herself or abusing substances. She believed she'd do anything to feel something other than how she was feeling in that moment.

When Sharon was diagnosed by a therapist as having borderline personality disorder, part of her felt great shame. She did some research online, and saw inaccurate information about the disorder being incurable. But then she met with a DBT therapist. She learned that BPD, when treated correctly, was not the terrible, lifelong sentence she had imagined. She realized she could learn to manage emotions that often felt unmanageable. She could improve her relationships, and this disorder did not mean she was broken and unlovable. What a relief.

What Is BPD?

So what is this thing called BPD? Folks with borderline personality disorder often struggle with emotions, impulsive behaviors, their sense of identity, and their relationships.

The *Diagnostic and Statistical Manual of Mental Disorders*, fifth edition (*DSM-5*) is the handbook listing the criteria of various mental health disorders, including BPD. Please be aware that these criteria can often feel discouraging and judgmental; don't let them be a referendum on who you are.

According to the *DSM-5*, five of these nine symptoms need to be present to receive a diagnosis of BPD:

- Frantic efforts to avoid abandonment, either real or imagined

- Unstable and intense interpersonal relationships, with relationship partners being alternatively idealized or devalued

- Unstable self-image or sense of self

- At least two areas of impulsive behavior (e.g., binge eating, spending, sex, substance abuse, risky driving) that can be damaging to one's health

- Suicidal gestures, or threats, or self-harming behavior (cutting, burning, or hitting oneself are most common)

- Marked reactivity of mood

- Chronic feelings of emptiness

- Anger that is inappropriate, intense, or difficult to control

- Transient, stress-related paranoid ideation (feeling threatened, persecuted, or conspired against or suspicion regarding the motives or intentions of others) or severe dissociation (feeling disconnected from one's thoughts, feelings, memories, or sense of identity)

If you find that list discouraging, you're not alone. Without training, understanding these criteria can be challenging. In fact, a number of my clients have felt the criteria have been weaponized against them by family members, health care providers, and even therapists, all of whom lack a deep understanding of what living with BPD is really like. One referred to it as "a comprehensive listing of why I am a bad person."

There's no reason to stay stuck in this outdated conception of BPD. In the groundbreaking book *Cognitive-Behavioral Treatment of Borderline Personality Disorder*, Marsha Linehan, the creator of DBT, reorganizes these criteria into what many who treat folks with BPD view as a much more understanding and comprehensive model. Linehan describes five areas of dysregulation—that is, problems regulating—that folks with BPD tend to struggle with:

- **Emotional dysregulation:** Rapid changes in moods and difficulty regulating emotions

- **Interpersonal dysregulation:** Intense and sometimes chaotic relationships and fears of being abandoned

- **Behavioral dysregulation:** Impulsivity that can be damaging to oneself, and/or suicidal or self-harm behavior

- **Self and identity dysregulation:** Not having a very clear sense of self; feelings of emptiness

- **Cognitive dysregulation:** Having suspicious thoughts about people's motives, or how they feel about you; and/or feeling like you are not in your body or feeling numb, spaced out, or checked out

I and many other professionals really feel that this way of looking at BPD—as a disorder of dysregulation—is an accurate description of the issues that folks with BPD cope with. Throughout this book you will gain greater awareness of how to shift from dysregulation to regulation, which means being better able to manage your emotions, behaviors, thoughts, relationships, and sense of self, rather than being managed *by* them. You'll work on developing skills to cope with challenging emotions so that you don't engage in unhelpful behaviors, like drug or alcohol use, that may provide relief in the moment but create problems in the long term.

The History of an Evolving Diagnosis

There's been controversy over the years over the term "borderline" in particular as an outdated and stigmatized term, a shorthand way for therapists to designate clients as difficult and unlikely to get better. Likewise, "personality disorder" can imply that someone is flawed, that the problem is within them and not influenced by environment and genetics. It also suggests a condition that's long-term and unchanging. There is some debate over whether BPD should even be classified as a personality disorder, or if it's a mood disorder, an identity disorder, or even a complex form of post-traumatic stress disorder.

To understand why BPD is one of the most controversial and misunderstood diagnoses in the mental health realm, let's take a quick trip through history. In the 1950s, mental health treatment—primarily psychoanalysis, which had been developed by Sigmund Freud—became more commonplace for people suffering from "neurosis," a term broadly used for difficulties in life associated with anxiety and depression. The other category of mental illness was considered "psychosis," which meant that the person was out of touch with reality, suffering from hallucinations and/or delusions. At that time, this was not considered treatable.

But a third group of patients did not quite fit into either category. These folks were in touch with reality, but usually did not benefit much from psychoanalysis. The symptoms they were troubled by were pretty much consistent with what we now consider BPD. These patients began to be referred to as "on the borderline" between neurosis and psychosis. Thus began the notion of "borderline personality disorder" as a condition that was just not going to get better. This assumption has since been proven wrong.

The diagnosis continues to evolve, with many treating professionals and affected persons lobbying for a rethink of the official diagnostic criteria and a new name. More and more treatment professionals are becoming educated about how to treat BPD and are learning to not place shame or blame on folks with the disorder for having the disorder. We've come a long way. And we still have quite a way to go. (Hey! That's a dialectical statement. You'll learn more about those later.)

The Relationship between BPD and Self-Harm

Suicidal thoughts, attempts, and self-harm behaviors are pretty common among folks who have been diagnosed with BPD, but just because they are common behaviors, it doesn't mean they aren't to be taken seriously.

Let's define our terms: Suicidal ideation means thinking about ending your life. A suicide attempt is an act you do in an effort to deliberately end your life. In contrast, self-harm, also called non-suicidal self-injury or self-injurious behavior, means deliberately hurting yourself but without an intention of dying.

You may wonder why these behaviors are so prevalent among people with BPD. The most common reason cited through research is to achieve relief or escape from emotional pain.

If you have engaged in or had urges to engage in these behaviors, you have probably noticed that when emotions hit, they hit hard. You may have been so overwhelmed that you were tempted to do something—anything—to make those emotions stop. The fact of the matter is that extreme behaviors tend to work to reduce emotional distress. But only in the short term. There's no question that the risks and long-term implications definitely outweigh this relief. Nevertheless, in light of being overwhelmed by emotion, we can understand that these behaviors seem to make sense in the moment.

Another reason why people with BPD may self-harm is because of feelings of numbness, emptiness, or being dissociated (disconnected from their body). If you have experienced these feelings, you know how deeply uncomfortable they are. Sometimes a person in that state will self-injure to feel something else instead.

Other reasons for suicide attempts or self-harm behaviors include efforts by someone to communicate emotional pain to others that they have no words to describe, or to punish themselves.

I can't emphasize this enough: It is very important to seek help from a professional therapist if you engage in these behaviors, to learn skills to manage them. If you are actively suicidal, reach out for help immediately. The Resources section (page 158) contains more information on who you can reach out to for assistance. In addition to this, in chapter 7 (page 137) you will find a safety plan you can create to prepare for a crisis.

Please try not to be discouraged. I have had the great pleasure and honor of seeing firsthand how effective treatment transforms the lives of folks who have struggled with these impulses and behaviors. If you have engaged in these behaviors or have had impulses to do so, remember, you can benefit from treatment, too.

Overcoming Stigma

Unfortunately, BPD is a diagnosis that remains surrounded by stigma both from mental health professionals and society in general. Common stereotypes paint BPD patients as dramatic, manipulative, and attention-seeking.

As you read earlier, in the not too far-off past, treatment providers did not know how to treat the disorder, leading them to categorize these patients as "resistant," which is often construed as saying that they did not want to get better. Although very effective treatments for BPD have since been created, it can take a while for new ideas to reach everyone who needs them. Unfortunately, even now, and even among health care professionals, BPD is frequently misunderstood. And, consequently, many mental health professionals are reluctant to treat people with BPD.

It's also true that without proper training and education, therapists can cause more harm than good when diagnosing and treating the disorder.

Stigma surrounding BPD can lead to misdiagnosis, for example. Some therapists have been trained in the old, one-size-fits-all stereotypical portrayal of BPD, a view that Hollywood films have frequently latched on to. One-sided, oversimplified representations of people with the disorder are often great dramatic fodder but don't accurately represent the average person with BPD. And if you have looked up BPD on the Web, I suspect you have seen firsthand some pretty negative information.

Partially because of untrue and irresponsible stereotypes, I have had many clients with BPD who were not diagnosed by previous providers because they were "just too likable" to have the disorder. Those with borderline personality disorder are often mistakenly diagnosed with bipolar disorder or major depressive disorder. And because the treatments for these illnesses are very different, this inaccurate diagnosis can cause at the very least a delay in getting effective treatment or, at worst, great harm.

For all those reasons, it is crucial to find a clinician who is up to date, trained, and knowledgeable about borderline personality disorder and the current treatment standards.

It's particularly important to be aware of the stigma surrounding behaviors like self-harm and suicide. Many people, including some therapists, are not well-qualified to understand and help individuals who engage in self-harm or suicidal ideation. Due to their fear of the consequences, and the fact that they might never have experienced these urges themselves, clinicians and others may find these behaviors frightening and confusing. But research has shown that getting others' attention, or manipulating them, is not the primary reason people with BPD engage in these behaviors. In any case, isn't seeking help or attention a basic part of being human? Why should that be pathologized for folks with BPD?

I'm happy to say that things are changing. As effective treatments have been developed and the good news about the outcomes of effective treatment get more notice, more and more people are shedding the stigma that surrounds the BPD diagnosis. And as you're about to learn, not only can individuals overcome BPD, there are some pretty great things about being a big feeler, too.

Your Strength, Resilience, and Empathy

As BPD symptoms can be confusing, you may have experienced some judgment or rejection from people around you, even those closest to you. Of course, you know that the symptoms of BPD can be challenging to deal with. But I have been hard-pressed to find a person with BPD who did not also have great gifts. These often include being:

- **Intuitive and perceptive.** Folks with BPD often are very sensitive to their surroundings and to the emotions of others.

- **Passionate.** When a person with BPD loves, they love hard. They are committed and loyal to those they care for. They are excited about ideas and plans. This passion is often found inspiring by others, and many people with BPD are highly charismatic.

- **Caring and highly empathic.** Because folks with BPD are very emotionally sensitive, they are passionate about causes and helping others. Many are activists or volunteers, or work in helping professions.

- **Resilient.** Just dealing with and managing the stress of overwhelming emotions on a daily basis points to resilience and ingenuity.

- **Bold.** Although impulsivity is a BPD trait that is often considered negative, it can mean being bold, courageous, and having the willingness to speak one's mind.

- **Creative.** Many people with BPD channel their intense emotions into creative endeavors. People with BPD often express their emotions through music, art, performance, and writing.

Remember, you're more than your symptoms! Everyone has strengths, and you're no exception.

People Experience BPD Differently

It is important to remember that although many people have BPD, each individual's experience of the disorder is different. BPD presents in a multitude of different ways. Some people turn their symptoms inward, and it is unusual for others, except perhaps those very close to them, to know that they suffer. Sometimes this is described as "quiet BPD." Others express emotions in a big way that makes it clear what they are feeling. Some people have had such difficulty in their experiences with emotion they become almost emotion-phobic and do anything to avoid feelings, situations, and people that spark emotion. For example, if displays of anger have created difficulties for them, they will try to suppress or deny anger and strive to always display a calm exterior despite their internal turmoil. Some folks with BPD when distressed will blame other people for their distress; others will blame or criticize themselves.

Some Common Experiences of People with BPD

Earlier in this chapter we reviewed Marsha Linehan's concept that people with BPD cope with difficulties in five different areas: emotional, interpersonal, sense of self, cognitive, and behavioral. Let's take a closer look at how each of these types of dysregulation are experienced.

Emotional

Emotional dysregulation involves the emotions feeling out of control and intolerable. You may find that your emotions are strong, sudden, and rapidly changing. Additionally, you may find yourself tempted to engage in behaviors that may temporarily relieve these feelings but that may not be consistent with your long-term goals.

Interpersonal

Relationships can sometimes be turbulent and chaotic when interpersonal dysregulation is present. When things are great with another person, they are really great. But when something goes wrong, you may feel devastated, hurt, and certain that the relationship is beyond repair. You might also fear being abandoned by those you care about. Sometimes this fear might create urges to engage in behaviors that might actually result in being abandoned. Excessive text messages or phone calls, or pleading or clinging to someone when they request space, are just a couple of examples of that.

Sense of Self

Self-dysregulation presents as a sense of emptiness, loneliness, or boredom. Or there can be confusion about your traits, beliefs, and purpose in the world. As you spend more time with certain people, you may find that your values, interests, goals, and even your identity change to align with theirs. Even if you try hard to fit in, you may still feel alone and excluded no matter what you do.

Cognitive

Simply put, cognitive dysregulation means problems in thinking. Sometimes you may have a black-and-white mindset, or you think in an all-or-nothing manner. Particularly when emotions are high, you might perceive people as either all good or all bad, rather than seeing them as both flawed and wonderful. In another form of cognitive dysregulation, you may feel as if the world around you isn't real. This is called dissociation. Lastly, some people may feel paranoid, believing that others are judging them negatively or attempting to harm them. It is possible that you may doubt the motives of people who you know care about you.

Behavioral

Behavioral dysregulation is the inability to control behaviors triggered by big emotions. When emotions feel too intense, you may have urges to harm yourself or engage in various impulsive behaviors, including drugs, alcohol, spending, gambling, eating binges, unsafe driving, or unsafe sex. You might feel compelled, when in high emotion, to plan suicide or make threats because it feels there is no other way to deal with the pain you are experiencing at the moment.

Potential Causes of BPD

Genetics and life experiences are likely contributing factors for developing BPD. Many researchers look at BPD through the lens of what is called "biosocial theory." The biological or "bio" part of the theory emphasizes that some people are just born more sensitive than others to emotions. For such people, emotions happen more often, feel stronger, and last longer. And these people have a harder time than others returning to baseline after experiencing intense emotions.

A biological predisposition toward impulsive behavior may also be present. It may be difficult for people with that predisposition to control their behavior, even if it causes problems. They might struggle to consistently achieve goals and control behaviors because moods get in the way.

An invalidating and ineffective social environment can make it difficult to regulate emotions, according to the "social" component of biosocial theory. An invalidating environment means that caregivers and others ignore the emotions of the emotionally sensitive person and do nothing until behaviors spiral out of control and ask or demand a change in emotional reactions without providing them with the tools to make this possible.

The people who contribute to an invalidating environment are generally not trying to harm; instead, they may not know how to help, or might not realize how important it is to understand and respect emotions, or may be struggling themselves, feeling overwhelmed and lacking in assistance. Sometimes there's a poor temperamental match between the emotionally sensitive person and the people closest to them—they just don't speak the same language. In any case, the emotionally sensitive person can end up believing their emotions don't make sense, are bad or wrong, and that help can only be obtained when emotions are out of control.

And the higher an individual's emotional sensitivity, the more likely they won't feel validated by their environment, leading to even stronger emotions.

Why Can BPD Be So Hard to Manage?

Drawing on her work with people with BPD, Marsha Linehan has described folks with untreated BPD as being akin to emotional burn victims. If you have BPD, every sensation and emotion can be painful to the point of intolerability. Your high level of emotion and difficulty tolerating distress can cause relationship turmoil, fears of being abandoned, and intense reactions when you think you might be being judged by others. You may be highly critical of yourself or others. And as we noted earlier, other people may not understand how to help or haven't taught you the skills to manage these emotions.

Is it any wonder that this disorder is often misunderstood? But, please remember, there is great cause for hope in the wake of a BPD diagnosis. As you will learn throughout this book, there are evidence-based skills that are highly effective. These skills can greatly improve your life and your relationships and result in greatly reduced dysregulation.

You Are Not Alone

It might surprise you to learn how common borderline personality disorder (BPD) actually is. Recent research indicates that 1.6 percent of U.S. residents live with BPD, which equates to around 4 million people. Women account for 75 percent of those diagnosed with BPD in the United States. However, it has been suggested that BPD diagnosis is biased based on gender. Males with BPD may mistakenly be diagnosed with post-traumatic stress disorder or major depression.

So if you have a BPD diagnosis, not only are you far from alone, it can be really helpful to get support from others who also have the diagnosis. Every day, I am inspired and filled with admiration for the many people who help those who struggle with dysregulation and for the organizations that support them. Please reach out to them. The groups are often staffed by people in recovery from BPD and those who love them. After reading the list of the positive qualities that can be associated with having had BPD, you may rightly expect that they are a pretty terrific bunch of people. You'll feel understood, hopeful, and less isolated. I've included a number of these organizations in the Resources section (page 158).

People Do Improve with Treatment

When someone struggles with regulating emotions, behaviors, and relationships, it can be hard to believe that life will not always be this way. You might think "Things may change for others, but not for me." But there's hard data to indicate BPD is treatable, not a life sentence.

A number of therapies have been proven effective for BPD, including dialectical behavior therapy (DBT), mentalization-based treatment (MBT), and transference-focused psychotherapy (TFP). Every day, new treatments are being developed and research is being conducted. A BPD diagnosis doesn't mean that someone will have to live with the symptoms forever.

A 2015 research study indicated that after a year of treatment with a comprehensive DBT program, 77 percent of people no longer met the criteria for BPD. That's hugely encouraging for a disorder that not too long ago was considered to be untreatable!

In this chapter you've learned a lot about BPD, its history, and its prognosis. With this understanding, you've taken a big step toward managing your symptoms. And there's lots more to come. As we move forward, it will be helpful to keep in mind:

- BPD, as it stands currently, is a disorder characterized by difficulty managing emotions, behaviors, sense of identity, and relationships. It does not mean you are a bad person.

- BPD has a history of being stigmatized, but with increased research and development of new treatments, people struggling with the disorder are going on to share their gifts with the world.

- Self-harm and suicidal behaviors are common to the disorder. See the Resources section (page 158) if you need help with those issues.

- You are not alone, and people with BPD absolutely can improve with treatment. Don't give up. There is hope!

CHAPTER 2

DBT for Lasting Change

Now that you have a deeper understanding of borderline personality disorder—and we've cleared up the misconceptions about it—it's time to talk treatment. We're going to take a closer look at dialectical behavior therapy (DBT), the well-researched and effective treatment for BPD that we touched on in chapter 1. We'll examine the underpinnings of DBT and talk a bit about the different skills that comprise the therapy. We'll also talk briefly about other evidence-based treatments for BPD and discuss what you can expect as you journey further through this book.

Cassie's Story: Finding the Right Help

Cassie had started to really hate going to therapy. She would talk about her life and her problems, and sometimes it helped her feel better for a bit. But other times, she would talk about something painful and come away feeling worse than before. In some sessions, when her life had calmed down a bit, her therapist might have some suggestions for how to make things better. But by the next week another crisis came up and attention had to be paid to that.

It felt like progress would never occur. And when Cassie mentioned she felt like she might want to harm herself, the therapist started to talk about hospitalizing her. Cassie had a friend who had been through that; it hadn't helped, and it had been very traumatic. Sometimes Cassie thought she saw fear behind her therapist's eyes, as if she had no idea what to do to help.

At their next session, Cassie's therapist noted that she had consulted with a colleague and felt that dialectical behavior therapy could be a really effective treatment for her. Her therapist encouraged Cassie to reach out to several DBT therapists who she knew provided good treatment. Cassie initially felt a bit rejected, but after some time with a new therapist, she knew DBT was the right path for her. Her new therapist got it! She didn't seem overwhelmed by her problems and was able to break them into bite-size chunks that made progress seem possible. For the first time in a long time, Cassie felt hope.

Diving Deeper into DBT

So far we've touched on dialectical behavior therapy (DBT), but what exactly does it involve? As mentioned, DBT is an evidence-based treatment developed by Dr. Marsha Linehan. "Evidence-based" means there is extensive research supporting DBT's efficacy. In essence, DBT combines cognitive behavioral therapy (CBT) with mindfulness and acceptance skills. We'll explore what each of these concepts involves throughout this chapter.

Folks with BPD struggle to regulate their emotions, and this emotional dysregulation can result in behaviors that can hinder their ability to live the lives they want. DBT is all about identifying problem behaviors that get in the way of creating a life worth living, tracking and understanding those problematic behaviors, and ultimately replacing them with new, more effective ways of being.

Roots in CBT

As mentioned, DBT combines cognitive behavioral therapy (CBT; please pardon all the acronyms) with acceptance and mindfulness. But what does that actually mean? Let's start with a really simplified description of the theory behind CBT: If you change your thoughts (the "cognitive" of CBT) and behaviors, your emotions will change. And as your emotions change, your thoughts and behaviors will continue to change as well. Change is clearly the focus here in CBT.

That approach causes some people to feel invalidated. Many folks who struggle with regulating emotions, when faced with traditional CBT, can feel that the focus on change overshadows the difficulty of the problems being experienced. This can lead to a suspicion that the people who are trying to help them do not fully understand their situation. And that makes sense! It can be really hard to accept interventions and solutions when you think the person trying to help doesn't really get it.

So, in creating DBT, Marsha Linehan blended the helpfulness of CBT with components that would account for people's need to feel heard, accepted without judgment, and sure that their problems were taken seriously. These extra added components include validation of self and others, embracing acceptance, and increasing mindfulness. The big difference here is that DBT emphasizes the importance of balancing acceptance *and* change.

The Founding and Development of DBT

In the beginning, Marsha Linehan wanted to create a behavior-based treatment specifically for people who were suicidal and self-harming. However, the people she was treating did not feel validated when she tried to guide them in behavioral, change-oriented therapy. It didn't seem to them like she understood their pain and that she thought they were the problem.

So, Linehan switched gears and started to provide acceptance-oriented therapy. The patients felt more understood and validated. But this revealed a problem with focusing solely on acceptance. The clients felt adrift between sessions; they didn't have the skills or strategies to use from day to day to help themselves and improve their lives.

This is where Linehan's game-changing idea came into play. She decided to blend change-oriented and acceptance-oriented techniques. Bringing these together was absolutely revolutionary for the clients she treated and for the world of psychology. Linehan dedicated herself and her team to researching extensively to make sure this treatment worked. And because of this dedication to finding the most effective ways to help, the treatment continues to evolve based on the newest research findings.

Since its founding, DBT has gone on to help countless people around the world and is regarded as one of the most important scientific ideas of our time.

The Dialectic of Acceptance and Change

In developing her concept of balancing acceptance and change, Linehan initially had no idea that this embrace of opposites had a name. "Dialectics" is a complex concept that has influenced scientific and philosophical thought. It's a method of investigating by examining opposite ideas. (Remember when we said, "We've come a long way. And we still have quite a way to go," last chapter? That statement may seem contradictory, but both parts can be true.) Linehan decided to incorporate the word "dialectical" into the name of the treatment as it so effectively described the balance of acceptance and change that was helping the people she was treating.

So, how does balancing acceptance and change help a person with BPD, not just in therapy sessions but in real life? Being able to see the many sides of a situation is very helpful in reducing emotional dysregulation. Let's say I make a mistake of some sort. If I look at that from a solely change-oriented perspective, I might think that I cannot rest until that mistake is fixed, and that I must be exceptionally hard on myself to ensure that another mistake is not made. It may feel impossible to move beyond my feelings until this problem is addressed and solved. On the other hand, if I come at the same situation solely from an acceptance-oriented viewpoint, I might just shrug and say, "Oh well," eventually decide that my actions are meaningless, and become hopeless and unmotivated. However, if I come from a dialectical perspective, I can allow myself to accept that I am human and make mistakes while also working toward making changes and learning new things.

That balance allows me to much more readily regulate my emotions. When we feel stuck and believe there is only one way of viewing a situation, this can be seen as a lack of dialectical thinking. You can practice a dialectical approach by asking yourself in any situation, "What else could be true?" This simple question can often help us see ourselves, others, and life in general from a different vantage point. This ability to see multiple perspectives helps us feel less stuck, improves relationships, and helps us see multiple ways of solving problems.

DBT Skills for Acceptance and Growth

The skills that are taught in dialectical behavior therapy are grouped into four different modules (page 24):

- Emotion regulation

- Mindfulness

- Interpersonal effectiveness

- Distress tolerance

The left two of these are change skills, and the right two are acceptance skills. We'll explore what each of these modules involves in the coming pages—and in more detail still in chapters 3 to 6, each of which is each dedicated to learning the specific skills of each module, in sequence. To get us started, let's look at the handy diagram on the following page, which shows the modules and their short definitions.

Before you read on, it is important to know that DBT skills are not one-and-done. Often, to be truly effective in regulating your emotions you may need to use at least a few different skills in any situation. Think of DBT skills like a language: one or two words or phrases might suffice at times, but being able to fluently use a host of different skills is most likely to lead to success.

Change | Acceptance

EMOTION REGULATION

Understanding and managing intense emotions so that you are less vulnerable to them

MINDFULNESS

Being present and accepting the current moment without judgment

INTERPERSONAL EFFECTIVENESS

Getting your needs met, maintaining relationships, and increasing self-respect

DISTRESS TOLERANCE

Managing a crisis without worsening the situation and learning to accept reality as it is

Learning how to apply the skills, and knowing which skills to use when, takes time and experimentation. Sometimes a skill won't seem to make a difference in your emotional state or help you change a behavior. That is to be expected. It might be that you need more practice in that particular skill, or you might need to combine a few skills. Some of the skills are only intended to keep things from getting worse, not to change your emotional state. Occasionally, a skill might just not be for you (but please try a skill several times before you decide that).

Let's take a closer look at the four modules that comprise DBT.

Emotion Regulation

Emotion regulation skills help us label our feelings, regulate our emotions, and change how we respond. These skills help us be more effective at encountering and responding to negative emotions rather than being overwhelmed by them or trying to avoid them. DBT therapists often tell their clients that success is not always about feeling better but getting better at feeling. A key goal of the emotion regulation skills is to decrease vulnerability to negative emotions and increase engagement in and mindfulness of positive experiences and events. Skills in emotion regulation are change-oriented.

Interpersonal Effectiveness

The interpersonal effectiveness module focuses on getting what you need and maintaining your relationships while maintaining your own self-respect. Through this module, you will learn a variety of skills that, although they are not 100 percent guaranteed to get you what you want, increase the likelihood that others will take your requests or refusals more seriously. Skills related to inter-personal effectiveness are change-oriented.

Mindfulness

The core skill of DBT is mindfulness: paying attention to and accepting the present moment without trying to change it. The DBT skills require mindfulness because we must respond to what is actually occurring right now, not what we wish would happen or what we imagine will happen. Also, mindfulness plays a crucial role in accessing our wise mind, which supports our ability to be our best selves and make successful decisions. You'll learn more about this concept in chapter 3. The goal of mindfulness skills is not to change the current situation but instead to experience and tolerate it.

Distress Tolerance

There are two categories of skills in distress tolerance: crisis survival and radical acceptance.

Crisis survival skills are tools for navigating difficult situations without making them worse. They start with awareness that you're experiencing distress at a level that might lead to choices that do not align with your values and goals. Once you gain this awareness, you can choose from a menu of skills that can help you self-soothe and distract yourself from or improve on the present moment instead of acting immediately on unhelpful "crisis urges."

Radical acceptance, in contrast, focuses on how to cope when we are confronted with distressing situations that we are unable to change, either in the current moment or in the long term. As with mindfulness, distress tolerance skills are based on acceptance.

Using DBT on Your Own and with a Therapist

DBT is usually performed in the context of structured weekly therapy, between-session coaching from your therapist, a skills training group, and the therapist's participation in a weekly consultation group with other providers of DBT. This is generally referred to as "comprehensive DBT," the form of DBT that is considered evidence-based, meaning that it has been researched and found to be effective. This book is absolutely not comprehensive DBT. But that doesn't mean this book can't be helpful to you. Those of us who are DBT therapists are well aware that DBT can be expensive and hard to access. That's why this book exists. Extra props to you for your resourcefulness and DIY spirit! To provide some extra support, I have compiled lots of suggestions for self-help DBT resources as well as low-cost ways to learn the skills in more detail online. See the Resources section (page 158) for more details.

If you are in therapy with a non–DBT therapist, you may want to share this book with them. The therapists I know are always up for learning how to improve their efficacy and reduce their clients' suffering.

How Long Does It Take to Learn DBT?

Setting yourself up to be successful in DBT requires being mindful of the main dialectic of DBT: those two seeming opposites of acceptance and change. I think it's safe to say that the primary reason you are reading this book is that you are seeking change. There may also be people in your life who are eager for change. And I bet everyone wants that change to happen pretty quickly. However, I encourage you to take things slowly and provide yourself with lots of encouragement. Integrating dialectical thinking and DBT skills will take time.

When someone enters a structured DBT program, there is usually at least a six-month commitment. Even if you are working on your own with this book, I recommend taking your time, spending around a month to six weeks working through each of the modules, in sequence, as presented in chapters 3 to 6.

Learning how to apply the skills and knowing which skills to use when will take time and experimentation. Sometimes a skill won't seem to make a difference or help you change a behavior. That is to be expected. It might be that you need more practice in that skill, or you need to combine it with other skills, some of which you haven't yet learned. And some of the skills are only intended to keep things from getting worse, not to make a huge change in your emotional state. Remember, it's possible that a particular skill won't be right for you, but it's still worth trying it several times before making that decision.

Preparing to Get Started

Let's consider a few more things before moving on to part 2. There are some things you can do to help ease your journey into DBT:

Set up a schedule. Setting aside time each day and designating a quiet and comfortable place so you can concentrate will help you create a skills-building habit.

Be kind to yourself. It's useful to know that strong emotions may come up as you use this book. Being self-compassionate and encouraging is important. And don't be hard on yourself if you need to slow down or take a pause.

Sharing is okay but optional. You may or may not want to share with a trusted loved one that you are taking this journey so that they can provide you with support and encouragement. Just be sure to let them know the ways in which they can help. For example, as any of us who experience strong emotions can attest to, being told to "just use your DBT skills" in times of great distress can feel really invalidating. So, give your supporter some gentle dos and don'ts to help keep conflict and misunderstandings to a minimum.

Track your progress. Each of the upcoming skills-based chapters includes a tracker to help you document how often and how useful the skills are in practice. I encourage you to use the trackers; they will help you identify and build your skills repertoire as you go. Also, you may find that you want to create flash cards or other reminders of the skills to help build your fluency—see the Resources section (page 158) for useful tools.

OTHER TREATMENTS FOR BPD

Among the evidence-based treatments for borderline personality disorder, dialectical behavior therapy is the most well-known and most researched. This book focuses on DBT, but it is important to know that there are other promising treatments for BPD.

Mentalization-Based Treatment

This treatment involves learning to understand your own mental state, being able to differentiate your own thoughts and feelings from those of others, and being able to imagine the mental states of those around you. Understanding your own and other people's feelings enables you to understand the intent behind other people's behavior, and avoid responding impulsively and ineffectively.

Transference-Focused Psychotherapy

This treatment focuses on the relationship between therapist and patient. The patient's sense of identity is emphasized, and more stable and realistic experiences of both self and others are created. Identity-based problems with interpersonal relationships, self-esteem, and mood are addressed.

Schema-Focused Therapy

The goal here is to identify and change unhealthy ways of thinking. Schema-focused therapy assumes that when our basic childhood needs (such as safety, acceptance, and love) are under-met, we develop unhealthy ways of interpreting and interacting with the world. These "schema" are triggered when events in our current lives resemble those from the past. In response we may resort to the unhealthy patterns developed during our childhood rather than more effective ways of thinking and behaving.

What to Expect as You Journey through This Book

As touched upon earlier, difficult thoughts and feelings are certain to arise as you address your difficult emotions and skills for managing them. I cannot say this enough: being harsh, critical, or disrespectful to yourself during this process will not make things better. So many folks who have been diagnosed with BPD experience severe self-judgment and deep shame. And it is common to think that being cruel and unforgiving to ourselves is necessary in helping us to change behaviors we and others find problematic. This is *just not true*.

Being unkind and belittling toward yourself is actually more likely to cause an increase in the emotions and problematic behaviors you are seeking to resist. Have you ever felt like you didn't like something about yourself, judged yourself, and ended up feeling terrible? And then found yourself doing something that actually contributed to making the problem worse? For example, suppose you make a mistake at work, then tell yourself you are useless, and that makes you so upset that you lose track of time and are late for a meeting. Being compassionate toward yourself may have led to a different result.

I am absolutely aware that telling you to be kind to yourself is much easier said than done. What matters is that when you find yourself spiraling into shame about your behavior, judging yourself for having strong emotions, or feeling hopeless about your progress, please do your absolute best to treat yourself as you would treat someone you truly care about. That includes being encouraging rather than judgmental, making gentle suggestions to yourself rather than derogatory comments, and recognizing progress rather than focusing on how far you have to go.

It won't always be easy, but with practice you can get there.

KEY TAKEAWAYS

In this chapter, we've focused on effective treatments for borderline personality disorder with an emphasis on the effectiveness of DBT. We have talked about the skills comprising DBT and how they can help reduce the emotional and interpersonal dysregulation associated with BPD.

As we move forward, it may be helpful to keep in mind:

- Learning to think more dialectically, seeing that there are multiple ways of viewing any situation, is a key to success in DBT. Ask yourself, "What else could be true?"

- DBT contains four different skill sets: mindfulness and distress tolerance skills are focused on increasing acceptance; emotion regulation and interpersonal effectiveness emphasize facilitating change.

- Learning, practicing, and integrating new skills is hard work. Be kind to yourself!

- If therapy hasn't been helpful to you, it may be because your therapist was not trained in effective treatments for BPD. You are not broken or beyond help.

By paying attention to the present moment without judgment, I can reduce my suffering and better achieve my long-term goals.

PART II

DBT Strategies to Address BPD and Begin to Heal

Now that you have a strong understanding of both BPD and how DBT can help, it's time to get down to the business of learning DBT skills. The following five chapters will provide you with various resources to help you learn the skills. In each chapter you'll find prompts (writing assignments to complete in this book), exercises (written activities to complete in the space provided), and practices (ways to try out and learn your DBT skills in the real world). You might find it helpful to keep a journal, so you can record your thoughts and extended responses to the prompts, but that's optional.

The first four of these chapters will each focus on one of the four DBT modules: mindfulness, distress tolerance, emotion regulation, and interpersonal effectiveness. The final chapter will help bring it all together to empower you to keep improving your ability to regulate emotions and achieve your life-worth-living goal. Remember, go at your own pace, and as you move forward, feel free to review previous chapters whenever you need to.

CHAPTER 3

Practicing Mindfulness toward Presence and Acceptance

We'll begin our work together by exploring mindfulness, the first of the four DBT modules. As you learned in chapter 2, mindfulness refers to paying attention and accepting the present moment without trying to change it. The skills in this chapter will teach you how to become more mindful of the here and now and enable you to recognize and accept reality without feeling pressured to alter the situation. This chapter presents a range of useful activities designed to help you increase your core mindfulness skills so you can step closer to living better with BPD.

Jake's Story: The Path to Mindfulness

Jake felt like he was at the mercy of his emotions. He often found himself giving in to whatever urge he felt in the moment. It felt impossible sometimes to do anything unless he was in the mood to do it. And lately, that wasn't very often. His relationships were suffering, because he sometimes felt like he wasn't in the mood to interact with others. He had difficulty starting and finishing tasks because he often felt distracted. He felt like it was impossible to pay attention when his thoughts were pulled elsewhere.

Jake became really judgmental of himself. He called himself lazy and a "waste of space" and antisocial, among other things. Sometimes, he found himself getting angry at his girlfriend and saying things that he regretted and felt ashamed of later. He knew he had potential, but when he had all the feels, he just couldn't seem to do things that others found easy.

It wasn't until Jake discovered DBT that he began to practice simple mindfulness skills that he could use in his everyday life. He learned to stay in the present moment, to reduce his judgments of himself and others, and to regulate his emotions and do the things he knew were going to serve his goals for the future. In time, he finally felt like he had some control over his emotions and his life. He no longer felt compelled to do everything his emotions told him to do (or not do).

◗ Your Life-Worth-Living Goal

The phrase "life worth living" has come up in this book, and you'll notice it many more times as we move forward. In DBT, everything stems from the creation of a "life-worth-living" goal. When Marsha Linehan created DBT, she realized that helping people create their own version of a life worth living is an essential part of treating BPD, because it enables us to ride through tough times. We're strengthened by the possibility of a life that contains joy, connection, and achievement.

What does a life worth living look like? You might detail how and where you would like to live, what kind of relationships you would like to have, and what kind of impact you would like to have on the world. Note that this doesn't include things like learning coping skills or other therapeutic goals like that—we will get to those soon enough. This is your chance to dream a little and set up the "why" of doing all of the work of DBT.

Think about it and describe it in the space below. You can write in any format that you like. You might create a list of things that comprise a life worth living to you, or express your ideas in a few simple sentences. For example, "My life-worth-living goal is having a strong and loving relationship with my child, a safe and pleasant living space, caring and fun friendships, a stable income, and time to do creative things just for fun."

◗ Ways to Respond to Problems

When life presents you with a problem, DBT posits that you have a short menu of options: solve the problem, help yourself feel better about the problem, learn to tolerate the problem, stay upset, or make things worse. For this practice, bring to mind a problem you're currently struggling with, or one from the past, and consider which of these options might be best.

Solve the problem. In a nutshell: fix it. You can change the situation, leave the situation, make it go away, or burn it down, just to name a few ideas. In our chapters on emotion regulation and interpersonal effectiveness (chapters 5 and 6), you'll learn DBT skills that can be applied specifically to solving problems.

Help yourself feel better about the problem. A solution may not be possible or immediately available. But that doesn't mean you need to feel bad. In chapter 5, you'll learn how to regulate and change your emotional response.

Learn to tolerate the problem. By embracing acceptance, you can tolerate problems that are difficult or impossible to change. You'll be learning more about acceptance in this chapter, and also in chapter 4, when we work on distress tolerance.

Stay miserable. This is certainly an option. It involves using no skills. But you'll gain the skills that will help you handle things when you're feeling stuck and hopeless and don't even want to try. You'll learn about these in chapter 4.

Make things worse. Last on the list, technically this is an option, too. But you won't have to resort to this one.

For now, be mindful of these options; this habit will increase your success in DBT as you keep adding to your skill set.

❱ What Gets in the Way of Your Life-Worth-Living Goal?

Take a moment to pause and reflect on what behaviors, emotions, and thinking patterns get in the way of your life-worth-living goal. Then, answer the questions below. Be careful not to turn this into an exercise in self-loathing. State these barriers using only factual, descriptive language.

What thoughts get in the way?

Example: *I can sometimes think loved ones are trying to hurt me when they are not. I can sometimes have judgmental and dismissive thoughts about myself and my emotions.*

What emotions get in the way?

Example: *I can get very angry very quickly when I feel judged by someone else. I can feel shame at a very high level when I feel I have done something that others don't like.*

What behaviors get in the way?

Example: *When I am distressed, I tend to withdraw from others. This gets in the way of my goal of feeling connected and having a community.*

Example: *When I am upset, I sometimes hurt myself. This gets in the way of my goal of staying safe and treating my body with respect.*

❱ What Is Mindfulness?

Recall that mindfulness is being aware of the present moment, on purpose, without judgment, and without holding on to it. To be mindful is to present yourself to each new moment as it unfolds instead of wishing that things would happen as we want them to. Being mindful is the opposite of being on auto-pilot, doing things habitually, by rote, without thinking. Have you ever driven somewhere and forgotten how you got there? That's what being on autopilot is like. You weren't thinking of turning the key in the ignition, braking, pressing the accelerator, turning left, and turning right. You just did all these things and found yourself at your destination.

In some cases, doing things on autopilot can save you time and energy and allow you to focus on other things. Nonetheless, it can lead to trouble if you live most of your life on autopilot, acting out of habit and not paying attention to the present moment. This is especially true when it comes to emotions. When you practice mindfulness, you can notice what is really happening in the moment and choose how you react rather than reacting automatically. Meditation is a great way to practice mindfulness, but DBT has a strong focus on everyday mindfulness, on being aware of the present moment while carrying on with the business of our lives.

For this practice, give yourself a first experience of mindfulness by sitting comfortably for a short time and paying attention to the sensations of breathing. It really is amazing all that is going on just in the act of taking a breath. Noticing that is mindfulness in action.

HOW MINDFUL ARE YOU?

Take this quiz to cultivate your insight about your level of mindfulness. Check the column that applies for each statement.

	Rarely	Sometimes	Often
Forget what you are doing in the middle of a task?			
Finish a meal or snack without really noticing how much you have eaten?			
Find yourself staying up past your preferred bedtime?			
Lose focus while reading something and have to go back and reread?			
Need to rewatch part of a movie or show because you didn't pay close enough attention?			
Feel like you are on autopilot?			
Find that time passed and you can't really account for how you spent it?			
Need to ask people to repeat themselves during conversations?			

Give yourself five points for each time you answered "often," three points for "sometimes," and one point for "rarely." Then, add up your score:

1 to 18: You are often mindful. Read on to learn how to cement your skills.

19 to 29: You are pretty mindful, but have room for growth.

30 to 40: You're definitely in the right place. Regular mindfulness practice will help!

▶ Goals of Mindfulness

As you learn more about and practice more mindfulness, you are likely to experience its benefits. Nevertheless, you may sometimes feel less than motivated to be mindful. Here are some common goals and benefits that folks experience from continued regular mindfulness practice. Review these when you find your motivation lagging:

A reduction in suffering and an increase in happiness. Many people find their mindfulness practice provides a reduction in physical and emotional pain, an increase in joy and happiness, and improved relationships.

Increased ability to control your mind. People who practice mindfulness often report they are better able to focus and pay attention. They also report more ability to detach from upsetting or unhelpful thoughts, images, and sensations.

Improved ability to experience reality as it is. People practicing mindfulness find that as they gain more experience, they are better able to be effective in their lives. They benefit from seeing reality as it really is rather than filtering it through past experiences or fears of the future. People also find they are more present to their own lives and more present and connected in their relationships. Some experience an increased connection to the universe in its entirety.

Take some time to sit quietly in a comfortable place and think about the above goals. Imagine yourself experiencing these benefits and envision how your life would be different.

❱ The Three States of Mind

In DBT, there is a belief that humans tend to be in one of three states of mind.

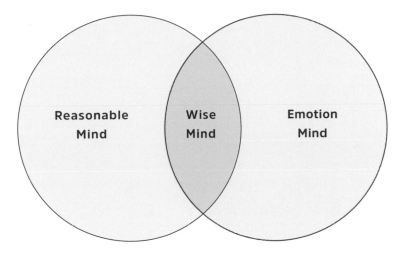

Reasonable mind is logical and task-oriented. It helps us get things done and follow the rules. But when it is not balanced by our emotion and wise minds, we are ruled solely by facts, rules, and procedures. Would you want to face a judge who didn't consider mitigating circumstances when issuing a ruling? Most likely not. Reasonable mind is great for solving math equations but not always great for understanding ourselves or improving our relationships.

Wise mind reflects the wisdom and set of values that each of us builds over the years. It's the ability to balance reason and emotion, but adds more: intuition, foresight, and "what really matters." We all possess wise mind, but some of us have a harder time accessing it than others. It can take practice. It is where we want to be when making important decisions.

Emotion mind is propelled by feelings, moods, and urges. No one would want a life without emotions, which would mean no joy or love. But when the emotion mind is not balanced by our reasonable and wise minds, our feelings are entirely in control. Nothing matters except our immediate desires and urges, which can lead to some risky situations. It's not the place we want to be when making vital choices that can impact our lives, jobs, and relationships.

▶ Exploring Emotion Mind

Take a moment to reflect on your experiences with being in emotion mind. Use the following writing prompts to increase your awareness of emotion mind and how it looks for you to be in that state.

What are some examples of times when you've been in emotion mind?

_____

_____

_____

What helps you identify when you are in emotion mind?

_____

_____

_____

How are emotions helpful to you?

_____

_____

_____

How is emotion mind unhelpful to you?

_____

_____

_____

▶ Exploring Reasonable Mind

Take a moment to reflect on your experiences with reasonable mind. Use the following writing prompts to increase your awareness of reasonable mind and what it looks like for you.

What are some examples of times when you have been in reasonable mind?

_____

_____

What helps you identify when you are in reasonable mind?

_____

_____

How is reason helpful to you?

_____

_____

How is reasonable mind unhelpful to you?

_____

_____

▶ Exploring Wise Mind

Take a moment to reflect on your experiences with wise mind. If your first thought is, "I don't think I have a wise mind," rest assured that everyone does! Wise mind may be tough to access at first, but these questions may help you find it more readily.

What are some examples of times when you've been in wise mind? If you think you have never been in wise mind, write about what you think that would look like:

_____

_____

_____

What helps you identify that you are in wise mind? If you feel you never have been, imagine what it would be like.

_____

_____

_____

How is wise mind helpful to you? Or how could it be helpful?

_____

_____

_____

◗ Accessing Wise Mind with Mindfulness

Wise mind can be accessed by paying attention to the present moment without judgment; in other words, by practicing mindfulness. A sense of calm in the center of the body is a sign of wise mind for some people. Others feel this calm in their heart area or between their eyes (this is sometimes called the "third eye"). Sensing wise mind in this physical way allows us to recognize when we are in this state, this way of being that allows us to access our knowledge, intuition, and inner wisdom. It can take some practice to regularly attain wise mind. Here's one way to try.

Try this meditation for a few minutes to gain insight about how you might experience a wise mind.

1. Sit in a comfortable position and take a few gentle deep breaths.

2. As you continue breathing, notice the slight pause at the top of each inhale.

3. On the out breath, notice the slight pause at the bottom of each exhale.

4. At each pause, allow yourself to feel the stillness within the pause. In that pause, you may find the feeling of being in wise mind.

5. Continue the practice for up to five minutes or for as long as you need to access your wise mind. If you are finding it hard, you can always try again tomorrow.

❱ The WHAT and HOW of Mindfulness

Being mindful is such an experiential activity that it can be challenging to teach and learn it. To understand and improve your ability to do it, you must do it. So as you learn and practice mindfulness-based skills, be patient with yourself, without judgment. You'll get there.

A few things to keep in mind:

Distractions are inevitable. The goal of mindfulness is not to have a clear head, to eliminate all thoughts. There will be distractions, and your brain will think thoughts. Brains work that way! When your mind wanders, gently bringing your attention back to mindfulness—without criticizing yourself—helps build the "muscle" of mindfulness. Thank you, distractions!

Relaxation isn't the goal. Mindfulness is not necessarily about relaxation. The purpose is not to relax, but that may be a nice side effect depending on the particular mindfulness practice you choose to participate in.

Here's a helpful way to think about mindfulness. According to Marsha Linehan, mindfulness includes three WHAT skills, that is, what we do when we practice mindfulness: observe, describe, and participate. We can only do each one at a time, and unless we are doing a practice specifically focused on one of these skills, we typically flip back and forth between them as we are being mindful.

In addition, there are three skills describing HOW mindfulness is done: nonjudgmentally, one-mindfully, and effectively. These skills are applied all at the same time.

PRACTICING THE WHAT SKILLS

Keep this checklist with you and use it to record the WHAT skills as you try them out over the course of a week (or however long you want). Choose a time and place to practice these skills—during a walk, while sitting on a park bench, on a break at work, or whatever's practical. Focus on one skill at a time, or move through the list however you prefer. Repeat and see how your skills grow. Go at your own pace and move on when you're ready. If you like, make copies of the checklist to use in the future as you continue your mindfulness practice.

Observe. You can observe your internal and external worlds by paying attention to your senses, emotions, thoughts, and body sensations. You can think of observing as watching without saying a word. Have you ever noticed how babies view the world? Despite taking in everything, they are not applying language to it. Try out these ways of observing and check them off as you go.

☐ Observe thoughts coming in and out of your mind (imagine your mind as a conveyor belt; let the thoughts roll past without engaging with them).

☐ Observe the sensations involved in your breathing.

☐ Find a small object and look at it closely, paying attention to each detail. Sit by a window or somewhere with a view. Watch the world go by.

☐ Notice the sounds around you and the spaces between the sounds.

☐ Listen to a piece of music. Feel the music in your body.

☐ When drinking a beverage, notice the smell as you bring the cup to your mouth each time you sip.

Continued on next page ➤

Describe. With this skill, it's important that you just use factual descriptors, not judgments. Only describe what can be observed. Remember that we can describe our own inner experiences but not the inner experiences of another. We might note when someone's facial expression includes a furrowed brow and down-turned lips. But only they can for sure say that they are angry.

☐ Practice your describing skills using the ideas below, and check them off as you go.

☐ Choose a small object. Describe that object in detail.

☐ Describe the behavior of a character in a movie without describing intentions, motives, or outcomes that are not directly shown in the film.

☐ Choose a political figure you are not fond of. Describe them in factual terms, without judgment.

☐ Working with another person, choose an object but don't show it to the other person. Ask your partner to draw the object merely from your description.

Participate. With this skill, you enter completely into the present moment and throw yourself completely into the now. When we participate, we let go of observing and describing and enter fully into the moment. Practice participating with some of these ideas and check them off as you go.

☐ Sing out loud.

☐ Make art.

☐ Go for a walk. Completely immerse yourself in the walk.

☐ Dance with all of your heart.

☐ Garden.

☐ Play a sport.

☐ Intently participate in a conversation.

▶ Leaves on a Stream

The purpose of this mindfulness practice is to help you observe your thoughts. Watching the thoughts is the goal, not reacting to or holding on to your thoughts. Learning to observe thoughts is really helpful if you are someone who can get caught up in worrying or ruminations.

1. Close your eyes and sit comfortably. Let your breath find its own gentle rhythm.

2. Take a moment to imagine yourself sitting near a stream. Create a picture in your mind of the stream by imagining its details.

3. Soon, you will notice thoughts forming in your mind as you spend some time by the stream. These thoughts may be about something on your to-do list or maybe about a conversation you had earlier in the day. When these thoughts arise, imagine placing them on a leaf. Then place the thought and the leaf in the stream and allow them to float away. Do this with each new thought.

4. Observe your experience while letting the thoughts float away.

Try to do this exercise for at least five minutes to give yourself time to settle in and let those thoughts float away.

PRACTICING THE HOW SKILLS

Remember that being mindful can be broken into two sets of skills: WHAT and HOW. We must skip back and forth between the WHAT skills, but the HOW skills can be done all at once. Think about the HOW skills as a way of being, or a stance you are taking while being mindful. Use this checklist to record these activities as you do them.

Practicing mindfulness nonjudgmentally. Practicing this skill means that you avoid judging people, places, things, situations, and so forth, as good or bad. Let go of "shoulds" and accept something simply as it is. However, remember that you will judge because you are human, and humans are designed to judge. So when it happens, take note of the judgment, let it go, and move forward. Try not to judge your judging! Another point to remember: Just because you decide not to judge, that doesn't mean you can't have preferences or likes and dislikes. It just means you are not defining people, places, things, and actions as inherently good or bad.

Try out some of these activities to practice nonjudgment, and check them off as you go.

☐ Notice and count your judgmental thoughts over the course of a day. You can do this using a golf counter or by making hash marks on a piece of paper.

☐ Choose a day to rethink your judging. When you notice yourself having a judgmental thought or making a judgmental statement, replace it with a nonjudgmental thought or statement.

☐ Identify something you dislike. Describe it using nonjudgmental words and tone of voice.

☐ Practice as much and as often as you can using nonjudgmental terms to describe events, the consequences of events, and your emotional responses to events.

Practicing mindfulness one-mindfully. To act one-mindfully is to be present, paying attention in this moment. And in this next moment. And in this next moment. And so on. It means you focus your attention on one activity at a time: washing the dishes, driving the car, walking down the street, taking a shower. Do this activity slowly, and do not let one movement go by without noticing it. Notice your breathing and your body movements as you do this activity. Nothing else matters other than what you are doing right now. Avoid multitasking.

Practicing acting one-mindfully with some of these ideas. Put a check next to those you complete. Feel free to come up with your own ideas, too.

☐ Be mindfully aware as you clean the house.

☐ Be mindfully aware while you sip tea.

☐ Be mindfully aware as you cook.

☐ Be mindfully aware as you wash your face.

Practicing mindfulness effectively. The key to being effective is to do what works in a particular situation. It means being skillful to achieve goals. It can mean choosing to be happy (getting what we want or need) over being right. It means playing the game you are in, not the game you wish you were in. Mindfulness strengthens all these things because it encourages us to see the present moment as it is. Try boosting your ability to act effectively with these practices, checking them off when you are done.

☐ Observe when you begin thinking about arguing about who is right or who is wrong, or what is fair or unfair, instead of doing what is necessary to achieve your goals.

☐ Be aware of when you become short with someone. Determine if this is the most effective behavior to use in this situation.

PRACTICING BEING NONJUDGMENTAL

We tend to judge things as good or bad, worthwhile or worthless, terrible or wonderful. All that judging can have a strong impact on our emotions. It can feed negative emotions, especially anger, guilt, and shame. And that can certainly interfere with our objective to be mindful in order to hear our wise mind.

Think about these statements:

- "That idiot driver in front of me clearly didn't know how to drive! You are taking your life into your hands every time you get in a car. It just isn't safe to drive anymore because people just drive recklessly and don't care who they hurt."

- "The person in front of me was driving really fast and pulled abruptly in front of me. I'm okay, but I really felt unsafe at the time."

Which created more negative emotion? Which was a more factual and accurate description of consequences? The first statement was judgmental; the second statement precisely and unemotionally described the situation and the consequences of the situation.

This exercise is intended to help you ease up on your judgments, aiming to increase your mindful awareness of reality and reduce your negative emotions. Here are the steps for letting go of judgments:

1. Practice noticing when you are judging something. Once you're watching for them, you may notice far more judgments than you thought!

2. When you find yourself passing judgment, ask yourself, "Is judging helping or hurting me?" If it's not helping, try replacing the judgment with:

   - Statements of fact: accurate descriptions of what really happened.

   - Statements of consequences: how the situation could be harmful or helpful.

   - Statements of preference: what you prefer or wish things were like.

With that in mind, try the following exercise to let go of a judgment of your own. First, identify a judgment you've made about yourself, someone else, or a situation.

Why do you want to let go of this judgment?

Continued on next page ➤

Replace your judgment with facts, consequences, or preferences. Write the new statement below. For example, replace "He's a jerk" with "He did something I did not like."

_____

_____

_____

_____

_____

How have your emotions changed as you have practiced being nonjudgmental?

_____

_____

_____

_____

Try following a similar process the next time you catch yourself making an unhelpful judgment in your day-to-day life.

▶ Practicing One-Mindfully while Walking

You probably don't pay a whole lot of attention to the act of walking. But it's a great opportunity to perform an activity one-mindfully. Because you will be intently focusing on the act of walking, please make sure you are somewhere safe when you do this. Here's how:

1. Start walking at your own pace. Depending on what is comfortable, place your hands on your belly, behind your back, or at your sides.

2. Be aware of how your foot lifts and falls with each step. Take note of the movement in your legs and the rest of your body. You may notice your body shifting side-to-side.

3. Whatever else captures your attention, note the distraction and then refocus your attention back to the sensation of walking. Your mind will wander throughout this activity; when it does so, gently nudge your mind back to the task at hand.

4. Wherever else your mind finds itself throughout the practice, come back to awareness of the physical sensations of walking. Notice your feet again touching the ground. Notice again the movements in your body with each step.

5. You can continue for as long or as short a time as you like.

6. Once you're ready to end your walking meditation, stand still for a moment. As you finish, consider how you might bring this kind of awareness into the rest of your day.

BEING EFFECTIVE

As discussed earlier, the mindfulness skill of effectiveness involves putting aside your current negative emotions in a difficult situation so you can act in ways more likely to help you meet your goal. Let's say, for example, that you feel you've been treated unfairly. Your emotion mind is screaming at you to let the person responsible absolutely have it. But that person is your boss, and you can't go off on him because you might be fired. So even though it feels important to confront him about his behavior, you are the one who will suffer, because it puts your job at risk. But if you recognize that your emotion mind is not helping, you can find a more effective solution, whether it's having a calm discussion, bringing a complaint to HR, biding your time while you seek a better job, or something else.

Here's an exercise you can use to guide yourself in being more effective in difficult circumstances.

Name a situation in which you feel you have been treated unfairly.

This situation makes me feel:

If I acted on those feelings, I would:

Rather than following what emotion mind is urging me to do, I could respond effectively by:

This could help my situation by:

❱ Loving-Kindness Practice

"Loving-kindness" is a meditative form of mindfulness that focuses on sending warm wishes to ourselves and to others. Data suggests that loving-kindness meditation increases positive emotions such as love, joy, gratitude, hope, and awe and reduces negative emotions. Here's how to do it:

1. Find a comfortable, relaxed posture, and take two or three deep breaths.

2. Allow yourself to sink into the intention of sending loving-kindness toward yourself. This can be difficult, especially if you tend to be hard on yourself. Do your best. Say to yourself: *May I be happy. May I be well. May I be safe. May I be peaceful and at ease.*

3. After directing loving-kindness toward yourself, bring to mind your loved ones, and then repeat phrases of loving-kindness toward them: *May you be happy. May you be well. May you be safe. May you be peaceful and at ease.* Allow yourself to feel positive sensations of loving-kindness.

4. As you continue the meditation, bring to mind other friends, neighbors, and acquaintances, and direct phrases of loving-kindness toward them: *May you be happy. May you be well. May you be safe. May you be peaceful and at ease.*

5. Now move to a person you feel angry with. Direct loving-kindness toward them: *May you be happy. May you be well. May you be safe. May you be peaceful and at ease.* This can help you release anger and resentment.

6. Now direct loving-kindness to all living beings: *May you be happy. May you be well. May you be safe. May you be peaceful and at ease.*

Take a few deep breaths. Enjoy the feeling of having sent loving-kindness to yourself and out into the world.

MINDFULNESS DIARY CARD

To start training your brain to be more mindful, set a goal to practice one or more mindfulness skills daily for the next week using this diary. Diary cards like these are an important part of keeping track of your progress in DBT. Use the following scale to rate the effectiveness of each skill and record the number on the card in the field that corresponds with the relevant skill and day of the week. Rating: 1 = Didn't help at all; 2 = Helped a little, I felt mindful for a while; and 3 = Helped a lot. Remember to keep trying all of the skills to build your mindfulness repertoire; it is important not to just write off a skill because it wasn't successful the first time.

	M	Tu	W	Th	F	Sa	Su
Ways to Respond to Problems (page 38)							
Exploring Reasonable Mind (page 45)							
Exploring Wise Mind (page 46)							
Accessing Wise Mind with Mindfulness (page 47)							
Practicing the WHAT Skills (page 49)							
Leaves on a Stream (page 51)							
Practicing the HOW Skills (page 52)							
Practicing Being Nonjudgmental (page 54)							
Practicing One-Mindfully while Walking (page 57)							
Being Effective (page 58)							
Loving-Kindness Practice (page 59)							

You've gotten a solid foundation in this chapter about the benefits of mindfulness for folks with BPD. You've practiced some mindfulness, learned about the three states of mind, and the WHAT and HOW skills. You've engaged in loving-kindness practice and gained some insight into which practices might become your go-to skills.

As we continue, it may be helpful to keep in mind:

- It is important to engage in mindfulness often, especially when you are not dysregulated, so that you can rely on your skills when things hit the fan.

- You can practice mindfulness anywhere at any time! Whatever you're doing, focus all of your attention on it.

- Remember to catch yourself when you are judging. Judging can result in an increase in emotions. By reducing your judgments, you can often reduce your suffering.

- Bottom line, mindfulness is the recipe for getting into wise mind, where we make decisions in line with our goals and values.

I can skillfully manage
my distress and avoid
giving in to crisis urges.

CHAPTER 4

Learning to Tolerate Distress and Painful Situations

Becoming better at tolerating distress and painful situations feels like a superpower for people dealing with BPD. When emotions are high, impulsive behaviors can follow. Getting through a crisis can feel impossible.

This chapter's focus on distress tolerance is going to provide skills to help you get through bad situations without making them worse. You'll learn about crisis survival skills that you can use when you are experiencing extreme distress. You'll also learn to accept situations that you can't change, whether right now or forever.

Trina's Story: Navigating Distress

Trina often felt like she was living in an emotional mine-field. No matter how hard she tried, she found herself at the mercy of her emotions. When a distressing emotion came along, she felt so overwhelmed that she had to do something to make the emotion stop. When she felt hurt by something someone said, she would get angry and lash out. That would feel great for a minute, but then she would feel ashamed and berate herself endlessly.

When she felt like a romantic partner might leave her, she would say anything to try to make them stay because her fear of being alone was so intense. But often her partner would be irritated by this and maybe end up leaving anyway.

Sometimes her emotions would become so intense Trina would engage in risky behaviors, like hitting her head against the wall to get some relief. It did ease the emotion in the moment, but she was afraid of what she was doing to her body.

Other people seemed to manage their lives just fine. Why couldn't she figure out how not to do these things that just seemed to push people away when she wanted more than anything to be close?

After learning about the distress tolerance skills contained in DBT, Trina was able to better navigate difficult situations without making them worse. She felt like she was no longer at the mercy of her negative emotions. And she finally felt some hope!

Using Crisis Survival Skills to Avoid Impulsive Behaviors

We'll begin this chapter by exploring some skills that are all about getting through challenging emotions and situations. During these situations, emotion mind can take control, and you might feel no other choice than to engage in these emotion mind urges. Being more mindful, learning about events that prompt distress for you, and regularly practicing crisis survival skills will all lead to being more able to resist these urges.

One important thing to remember here is that these strategies won't fix your problems. The main goal is to keep things from getting out of hand, to avoid unhelpful coping strategies like self-harm, suicidal ideation, yelling at someone, using substances, or other impulsive behaviors that might end up making things worse.

Sometimes crisis survival skills do help you feel a bit better. But not always. Remember that getting through the bad situation without resorting to unhelpful coping strategies or making the situation worse is the win. Also important: Crisis survival skills are not usually one-and-done actions. Being skillful in a crisis can require using more than one skill. In the next chapter, which is all about emotion regulation skills, you will learn ways you can change or reduce your vulnerability to negative emotions instead of just tolerating them.

WHAT IS A CRISIS?

For our purposes, we will consider a crisis a painful, stressful situation that feels like it needs to be resolved or escaped right now. As an example, suppose you have an argument with your partner, can't come to some sort of resolution, and then you're out of touch with each other for a while. Your emotion mind might be on fire, questioning whether the relationship has any chance of staying intact. All you want is to contact your partner and know all is well. But your partner has asked for space, and reaching out before they're ready might make things worse.

Yet every cell in your body is screaming for a resolution to the problem. It sure feels like a crisis.

One way to describe the level of distress we feel in a crisis is to use subjective units of distress, commonly referred to as SUDs. Learning to rate SUDs can be helpful to you, because doing so can help you assess when to use the crisis survival skills you are about to learn.

For this exercise, fill in the chart on page 67 to become familiar with how SUDs appear in your life. Remember in chapter 2 we talked about acceptance skills and change skills? Becoming adept at rating your SUDs can help you know when to use acceptance-oriented skills—like the distress tolerance techniques explained in this chapter—which are intended to be of most use when your level of distress is on the high side. When your SUDs are lower, you'll be more effective at using change-oriented skills, like the emotion regulation and interpersonal effectiveness skills coming up in later chapters. And keep in mind that mindfulness skills are all-the-time skills, but they are especially useful when SUDs are high.

Level of Distress	Situation That Might Create This Level of Distress for You
0: Living my absolute best life, absolutely no distress at all	
1: Doing great, all is well	
2: Minimal distress, things are pretty chill	
3: Mild distress, no interference in functioning	
4: Mild to moderate distress	
5: Moderate distress but can definitely function	
6: Moderate to strong distress	
7: Quite distressed, difficulty focusing, emotion mind set to take over	
8: Very distressed, difficulty functioning	
9: Extremely distressed, emotion mind is clearly in charge	
10: Highest possible distress, feeling completely out of control	

▶ The STOP Skill

The STOP skill is helpful at almost any level of distress, but is especially helpful when you find yourself at a SUDs level of 6 or above. You can remember the steps using the **STOP** acronym. Here's how it works:

Stop. Seriously, stop. Don't move! Physically freeze for a moment, before the urge to react takes over.

Take a step back. Take a step back, either physically or mentally or both. Take a few deep breaths. Do not let your urge to react take over.

Observe. Observe and describe to yourself what is really happening. State it out loud if necessary. No judgments, assumptions, or interpretations. Just the facts, please.

Proceed mindfully. Ask your wise mind what the best response might be. What outcome will you feel best about tomorrow or next week? (Implementing this might require a skill from an upcoming chapter.)

To develop this skill, practice STOP at times when you are not distressed or when your SUDs are at a 2 or 3 level.

CONSIDERING PROS AND CONS

This skill is to be used in advance of a distressing situation, when you are in wise mind. A completed pros and cons list is like a tip sheet from your wise mind on the preferred response to a possible crisis. This practice gives you a very well-rounded understanding of the problem behavior, as well as all of the pros of keeping it in check.

Here is an example: Your partner, yet again, has not called to say they are going to be late. Expecting them to be home on time, you make a really great dinner. You sit, and wait and wait. Finally, after dinner has gone cold, they arrive. Your crisis urge is to immediately let them have it. They just can't treat you this way!

Now suppose you had worked on a pros and cons list while your SUDs were still low. It might look like this:

	Pros	Cons
Giving in to crisis urges	*If I yell, they will understand how upset this behavior makes me.* *They deserve to feel bad for what they did.* *It will feel so good to get this off my chest.*	*I really care about them and yelling is going to cause a rift.* *Maybe there's some explanation for them being late.* *Yelling will make me look like I can't handle my emotions.*
Resisting crisis urges	*Presenting my point calmly will make me feel in control of my emotions.* *We are less likely to have a fight.* *They might hear why it is so important to me that they call.*	*I won't get the satisfaction of yelling.* *They might not understand how hard it is for me when they are late.*

Continued on next page ➤

Now you give this a try with one of your triggering situations. Remember to engage wise mind! First, describe the behavior you are tempted to express in a crisis situation:

....

....

Now, make your list.

	Pros	Cons
Giving in to crisis urges		
Resisting crisis urges		

Empowered with this information, are you better off giving in to your crisis urge or resisting it?

❯ TIPP Your Body Chemistry

When emotions are running high, our body's reactions can feel overwhelming. Fortunately, there are ways to lower the intensity of the emotion and release its grip on your body. We can use skills that activate the parasympathetic nervous system, the part of your nervous system that calms the body down so it can rest and digest. Doing this reduces the physical symptoms associated with stress, like rapid heartbeat, and eases you into a state where you can use other coping skills. In DBT, these are called the **TIPP** skills because they "tip" your body chemistry away from a fight-or-flight reaction and toward relaxation. The letters of the acronym can help you remember the techniques to use:

Temperature change

Intense exercise

Paced breathing

Paired muscle relaxation

In the following pages you'll learn how to try each of these out.

A temperature change can induce the "mammalian dive reflex" (think of an animal holding its breath underwater), which puts the parasympathetic nervous system into action, reducing the bodily arousal that often accompanies intense emotions.

Before you try this skill, check with your medical provider to be sure this is safe for you, especially if you have cardiac problems, suffer from an eating disorder, or deal with other medical issues (especially those related to your heart).

The first time you try this, you may want to measure your heart rate before and after to see the effect that tipping your body chemistry in this way can have on your bodily response. To check your heart rate, press two fingers over your radial artery, which is located on the thumb side of your wrist between the bone and the tendon. Count the number of beats in fifteen seconds. Multiply this number by four to calculate your beats per minute.

Rate your SUDs _____ and record your heart rate _____ .

To kick off this reflex, immerse your face in a basin or sink full of cold water (not colder than 50°F) and hold your breath for thirty to sixty seconds.

You can get the same effect by filling a zip-top bag with ice cubes or cold water, wrapping it in a damp paper towel, and holding it over your eyes and cheeks. Even a cold washcloth on your face may do the trick. To intensify the effect, bend over to mimic a diving position and hold your breath for 30 to 60 seconds.

Now check your SUDs _____ and record your heart rate _____ .

Try again if you see no difference in your SUDs or heart rate.

USING INTENSE EXERCISE

Engaging in intense cardio/aerobic exercise, followed by a cooldown, can de-escalate intense emotions like fear or anger. Ideally, for this to work try to exercise for twenty minutes or more. How intense should the exercise be? The official DBT recommendation is 70 percent of your maximum heart rate, but if you don't know how to measure that, simply aim for the type of movement in which you can feel your heart rate is up.

After the exercise, pay attention as you cool down and note what it feels like. As you cool down from intense exercise, the body is reregulating itself to a calmer state. Remember, you don't have to hit the gym, you can take a brisk walk, do jumping jacks, march in place, or even dance!

Keeping track of your exercise and the impact it has on your SUDs can be really helpful. If you have a goal to increase the amount of your exercise to improve your health, it may help you to know you are also helping regulate your emotions. Even if your SUDs are not high when you exercise, regularly exercising and increasing your heart rate can help reduce your day-to-day anxiety. Use this chart to document the effect that everyday exercise and activity has on your SUDs so that when a crisis hijacks your emotions, you'll know how much movement will calm you down.

Form of Cardio Exercise	SUDs Before	SUDs After

▶ Pace Your Breathing

Paced breathing is a great TIPP skill to get the parasympathetic nervous system online when faced with a distressing situation. Paced breathing involves regulating your breathing in a way that allows you to access maximum calm.

Inhaling activates the sympathetic nervous system, which prepares us for action when we're stressed. Exhaling activates the parasympathetic nervous system, which calms us down. The trick is to spend more time exhaling than inhaling, so your body will slow down, calm down, and relax. This is a skill you can practice in advance of difficult situations, training yourself to activate the relaxation response more readily when you really need it. Let's give it a go!

1. Find a comfortable position.

2. Breathe in slowly through your nose for a count of two to four seconds, letting your chest and lower belly expand.

3. Breathe out slowly through your mouth for a count of four to six seconds. As you do, purse your lips and make a swoosh sound. (If there are other people around, feel free to skip the sound.)

4. Keep breathing in and out in the same way for a few minutes or for as long as desired. If your mind wanders, gently redirect your focus back to the counting and breathing.

Once you get a handle on this, you can try to slow your breathing down to five or six breath cycles per minute for maximum effect. Keep practicing, and find the pace that works best for you.

▶ Paired Muscle Relaxation

This final TIPP skill pairs muscle relaxation with breathing to activate the parasympathetic nervous system response. For each step, tense a part of your body for about ten seconds. As you release the tension, breathe out and say the word "relax" (or any other soothing word) to yourself. If you do not have full sensation in your body, feel free to swap out any specific body parts mentioned for others that you can sense.

1. Find a comfortable position sitting or lying down.

2. Start by focusing on your hands and wrists. Make your hands into fists and tighten your arm muscles. Hold for ten seconds, then relax.

3. Clench your jaw, squeeze your eyes shut, and tighten your facial muscles. Hold, then relax.

4. Pull your shoulders up to your ears and tense the muscles in your upper back. Hold, then relax.

5. Tighten the core muscles in your abdomen. Hold, then relax.

6. Squeeze your buttocks, hips, and groin muscles. Hold, then relax.

7. Focus on your knees and thigh muscles. Hold, then relax.

8. Clench your calves. Hold, then relax.

9. Focus on your feet and ankles. Curl your toes and flex your ankles. Release and relax.

Check in with yourself after doing this practice. Where are your SUDs? Do you feel more at ease than when you began?

▶ Distract Yourself Using ACCEPTS

In the next few pages, we'll focus on the **ACCEPTS** skill and later the **IMPROVE** skill, which both provide you with more ways to tolerate distress in the moment to avoid giving in to crisis urges. These skills revolve around distraction, soothing, and doing things to improve your current moment. One caution is to participate in the activities mindfully; ruminating on worries or resentments while participating in the skill will not reduce your SUDs. Mindfully focusing all of your attention on the skill is the key to using it effectively. Another caution is not to use these skills to try and numb or avoid your emotions entirely. These are intended to be used to get through crisis situations, not to escape all emotions or to avoid life.

The first skill is ACCEPTS, which includes methods to distract yourself when your SUDs are high and so avoid engaging in destructive behaviors. It's helpful to test these methods to learn which are most effective for you. When using ACCEPTS techniques, use one to start, and if you find yourself struggling to resist crisis urges, move to another, and then another if necessary.

The acronym ACCEPTS stands for the following:

Activity: Throw yourself completely into a distracting activity. Read, watch TV, clean house, go for a walk, sew, play a game.

Contribution: Help someone else. Volunteer, make someone a gift, donate items, call or text a loved one. This has the benefit of not only distracting you but also making you feel good about yourself.

Comparison: There are two different ways to practice this. One is to compare yourself to those less fortunate than you. This can create an attitude of gratitude. For some people, though, this creates feelings of guilt or shame for feeling overwhelmed when there are people who have it so much worse. In that case, it might be helpful to compare how skillfully you are handling this situation now compared to how you might have handled it in the past, or how much better you are feeling now than you might have in the past.

Emotion: Try to elicit emotions opposite to the one you are feeling now. For example, it you are sad, try watching a funny movie. If you are anxious, try listening to soothing music.

Pushing away: Imagine building a wall between you and your emotional distress. Or visualize putting your concerns in a box and putting it away.

Thoughts: Use other thoughts to shift your attention away from the distressing situation. For example, try saying the alphabet backward; remember the lyrics of a song; do a crossword puzzle—anything that helps keep your mind busy until the crisis passes.

Sensation: Use strong physical sensations to distract from strong emotions. Take a hot or cold shower, hold ice cubes in your hand, smell an intense scent, or eat a piece of sour candy. Take care that the distraction isn't something painful or damaging.

PUTTING ACCEPTS INTO ACTION

Use this log to increase your awareness of which ACCEPTS skills are most helpful for you in distressing moments. Remember, even if your SUDs are the same after completing the activity, it was still a success if you did not give in to crisis urges. Note: You do not need to put a detailed description in the situation column; just a single word to describe is fine.

	Situation	Distraction Used	SUDs Before	SUDs After	Did I Give in to Crisis Urges? (Y or N)
Activity					
Contribution					
Comparison					
Emotion					
Pushing Away					
Thoughts					
Sensation					

▶ Self-Soothe with Your Senses

Using your available senses as a launching point, you can focus mindfully on soothing activities when your SUDs are high. Below are some ideas. Use the lines beneath each to add another example of how you can practice self-soothing with each sense.

Vision: Sit and watch a sunset or visit nature. Look at artwork or photographs.

....

....

Hearing: Focus intently on the sounds of birds chirping. Play soothing music. Focus on the sounds of water.

....

....

Smell: Enjoy scented candles. Bake some bread. Put on your favorite lotion.

....

....

Taste: Brew a cup of herbal tea, chew a piece of gum, eat something very mindfully.

....

....

Touch: Put on comfy jammies. Take a bubble bath. Pet your cat.

....

....

▶ IMPROVE the Moment

The "improve the moment" skill set offers a menu of options you can use to shift your focus by making your negative experience a more positive one. Here are the options, which make up the acronym **IMPROVE**.

Imagery: You can focus on the sights around you. You envision yourself in a peaceful place. You can imagine releasing stress from your body. Or see yourself coping extraordinarily well in a tricky situation.

Meaning: Make sense of the painful situation you are facing. Look for the positives in your current situation. Is there anything you can learn from this situation that you can use to help others?

Prayer: This could mean traditional religious prayer, or be viewed as accessing wise mind or turning things over to something greater than yourself. However you use this skill, ask for strength rather than for the situation to disappear.

Relaxing action: Many things can bring a bit of relaxation to a difficult situation. Perhaps a few deep breaths? How about a walk, some yoga, or a nice bath?

One thing in the moment: Whenever you are doing something, bring a mindful focus to it. Observe when your mind starts to wander to painful memories from the past or fears about the future. Instead, concentrate on the current task. Dishes need to be washed? Take note of everything: the bubbles and the warmth of the water. It will keep you from focusing on unhelpful thoughts.

Vacation: This doesn't mean packing your bags for Bermuda! Taking a short break from your current challenges is the idea. That means making a plan to return to real life, too. If you are going to take a one-hour breather, set a timer and commit to returning when the timer goes off.

Encouragement: Sometimes we all need some cheerleading. We can tell ourselves, "This is hard, but I can do it," "I am doing the best I can," or "This, too, shall pass." The important part is to talk to yourself the way you would to someone you love.

When you feel an increase in negative emotions, refer to the IMPROVE options and complete the following log for the option chosen. Start by describing the situation that triggered the emotion(s), and identify the activity you will do in response, or that you already did. Consult the previous pages for ideas regarding what activities you can use. Rate your level of distress *before* and *after* you engage in the activity.

	Situation	Activity Used	Distress Level Before (0 to 10)	Distress Level After (0 to 10)
Imagery				
Meaning				
Prayer				
Relaxing Action				
One Thing in the Moment				
Vacation				
Encouragement				

◗ Building Your Crisis Survival Tool Kit

A crisis survival kit is extremely helpful to have on hand when emotions are high and you think you might be at risk of giving in to crisis urges. Think back to the skills we have covered so far and think about your favorites. Choose a container for your kit, like a box, bag, or basket. Place the items that will enable you to use your skills inside the kit: a stress ball, your favorite scented lotion, a picture of your favorite vacation spot, a favorite magazine, a crossword book, essential oils, herbal tea bags, a favorite piece of candy. You can also include reminder lists and instructions for enacting crisis survival skills. And don't forget the pros and cons lists you have created—each acts as a note from your wise mind in a time when emotion mind is more prevalent. You may consider keeping your kit in a place where you have been tempted to give in to crisis urges in the past.

Lots of my clients keep kits at home, work, the car, and in other places, anywhere a need for skills might arise. Think of it as a creative exercise. For example, if you have found inducing the dive reflex through cold water or an ice pack to be helpful, how can you equip your kit for that? Some folks keep a plastic bag, a water bottle, and a few paper towels in their car. With a quick trip into a convenience store, they can grab a cup of ice at the soda fountain and have all the elements for inducing the dive reflex. Others keep instant ice packs on hand, the kind kept in first-aid kits. Hit them or squeeze them and they become cold.

Consider what your tool kit will look like and start gathering what you need.

▶ Practicing Radical Acceptance

A very difficult truth is that life can be unfair, and things don't always go how we would like. Sometimes it's small stuff, like traffic congestion or dropping your ice cream cone. And sometimes it's the really big stuff, like having been abused as a child or losing someone you love. This is where another distress tolerance skill set comes into play. Earlier in this chapter, you learned how to survive crisis situations. Now we're going to focus on situations that cannot be changed and how to accept them in order to reduce suffering.

Not accepting something doesn't make it unhappen. And accepting the facts of a situation doesn't mean we have to approve of, or like, what happened. You don't have to accept anything other than the facts of the situation. And you only have to accept right now. For example, you only have to accept that you weren't hired for that job, not that you are doomed to never work again.

Fighting reality is exhausting and pretty darned pointless. Rejecting what has already happened not only doesn't change reality, it adds all kinds of negative emotions to the pain we already feel.

Radical acceptance is a distress tolerance skill intended to keep pain from turning into suffering. The equation looks something like this: Reality + acceptance of reality = pain. However, reality + nonacceptance of reality = pain *and* suffering. Pain is plenty hard enough. Adding suffering to the mix makes it pretty unbearable.

Although pain can't be avoided, and you may notice a sense of sadness as you grieve what could have been, ultimately radical acceptance brings a sense of calm, centeredness, and peace.

▶ Noticing Nonacceptance

Being aware of your thoughts, feelings, and body when you do not practice acceptance can help you learn to move toward acceptance more rapidly.

Think of a situation you had or have trouble accepting. Choose something relatively minor rather than a huge life loss. For example, being stuck in traffic, having to wait in line, or some other minor life event that causes frustration and a lack of willingness to accept. Now, describe the situation below.

When faced with this situation, what thoughts did you notice yourself having?

What feelings did you have? Did their intensity increase or decrease as you found yourself continuing not to accept?

What body sensations did you notice?

If you were able to move toward acceptance in this particular situation, what did you notice changing about your thoughts, feelings, and body sensations?

❱ Turn the Mind

Radical acceptance isn't something you do once, about a specific situation, and scratch off your list. When faced with a difficult situation, we often accept it, then suddenly find that we are no longer accepting. For example, ever lost your wallet? You check everywhere. And then you decide to accept that it is gone. But you find yourself checking again and again. Why? Because acceptance is hard. So, you accept for a bit, then go back to looking for your wallet again. And it's even harder for a more serious situation. At first you are accepting, and then you find you are not. This is where the practice of turning the mind comes into play. When having difficulty accepting, envision turning the mind to move yourself toward acceptance. Here's how:

1. Think of a situation you are struggling to accept.

2. Imagine that you are at a fork in the road. The path on the left leads toward nonacceptance, the one on the right leads toward acceptance.

3. Imagine yourself turning toward the path of acceptance.

4. Turn your mind toward acceptance.

Try this first with some situations that are difficult to accept but that have relatively low stakes. You can bring a past situation to mind or try it the next time life throws you a curveball. As the technique becomes familiar, apply it to bigger challenges.

▶ Willingness and Willfulness

What if you still have trouble accepting reality, despite trying to turn your mind? That's part of being human; we all experience it. It can be difficult to accept the cards life deals us, but getting upset or threatening to quit the game doesn't change the cards you get.

In DBT we call refusing to accept the cards you are dealt "willfulness." Accepting and playing the cards you get, even when you don't like them, is "willingness." Willingness is listening to wise mind and doing what is needed in each situation. Willfulness is giving up, wanting to be in control of every situation, demanding that things change immediately. Being willing to accept something does not mean you like or approve of it. Often it's the first step to making changes. Let's say you want to make changes to society. Just standing there and demanding change simply doesn't work. Accepting that society is broken and that one needs to work incrementally with others to improve things might result in change over the long term.

Use the lines below to reflect on your experiences with willfulness.

Describe a time you noticed yourself being willful, not accepting reality, and being ineffective with skills use.

....

....

Describe how being willing to accept the situation might have changed your emotions.

....

....

Describe how being willing to accept the situation might have changed your behaviors.

....

....

▶ Using the Body to Accept Reality

Virtually all of us have seen a statue of the Buddha. He looks pretty relaxed, right? That's partly because of two things: his sweet, soothing facial expression, and his open, upward-facing hands. With this image of the Buddha in mind, try practicing the half-smile and willing hands.

The half-smile is a way of reflecting to yourself that you accept reality. Emotions are partially controlled by facial expressions; the brain and the facial muscles are closest to each other and communicate very quickly. So changing your expression just might change your emotion. In other words, if you can adopt a serene face, you can actually *feel* more serene.

Here's how to half-smile:

1. Relax your face, neck, and shoulder muscles.

2. Then, just slightly raise the sides of your lips. It won't be noticeable to anyone but you; the expression tends to register to others as an expression of neutral interest. You are not smiling at anyone else. You are smiling at your brain. "Hey, brain, all is well. We're good."

"Willing hands" is another way of physically demonstrating to yourself that you accept reality. Open your hands, palms up, letting your fingers relax. This is a very open posture, good for embracing the opposite of anger.

❿ Mindfulness of Current Thoughts

Noticing and radically accepting thoughts is important for regulating emotions. Being able to observe thoughts as just thoughts, rather than treating them as reality, provides distance from them and reduces emotional reactivity. Here's how to handle your thoughts instead of letting them overwhelm you:

1. Find a comfortable position. Take a moment to settle into your body.

2. Take a deep breath or two.

3. Observe whatever thoughts come. Notice they can come as waves. Just let them happen; don't suppress or judge them. Don't hold on to them, either.

4. Adopt a curious mindset. Observe but don't evaluate your thoughts. Ask where they might come from, without overanalyzing.

5. Recognize these thoughts as mental events. Remember, you are not your thoughts.

6. Remind yourself of times when your thoughts were very different.

7. Allow the thoughts to come and go.

8. Try playing with your thoughts. Say them in the voice of a cartoon character, sing them, or pretend they are bumper stickers on cars driving by.

9. Remind yourself that a thought is just a thought.

Practice this regularly so you can more easily call on the skill when you need it.

▶ Reflections on Distress Tolerance Skills

Making the choice to use distress tolerance skills can be tough. When emotion mind is in control, it can make so much sense, at the time, to go with emotion mind urges.

When emotion mind is threatening to take over, it can be helpful to remind yourself of your "whys," your longer-term goals that giving in to emotion mind and crisis urges make less likely to happen. Use this space to write the reasons why your efforts to resist crisis urges and use skills to manage emotions are important. Remember to engage wise mind for this.

When faced with a difficult situation, I will use skills rather than giving in to crisis urges because:

When faced with strong emotions, I will use skills rather than giving in to crisis urges because:

When using skills is difficult and I just want to give up, I will use skills rather than giving in to crisis urges because:

Congratulations to you on choosing skills rather than giving in to crisis urges. Often, it's hard work to be skillful, especially in the beginning. Skills will become more easily accessible over time as you use them more and more. Your courage, commitment, and effort are to be commended!

DISTRESS TOLERANCE DIARY CARD

Using distress tolerance skills regularly is a big part of coping with difficult situations and emotions and not making things worse. Set a goal to practice one or more distress tolerance skills each day in the coming week. Use the following scale to rate the effectiveness of each skill on the day of the week you tried it. Rating: 1 = Didn't help tolerate distress at all; 2 = Helped tolerate distress a little so that I could cope for a while; and 3 = Helped a lot; I tolerated distress and did not give in to crisis urges. Remember to keep trying all of the skills to build your distress tolerance tool kit; it is important not to just write off a skill because it didn't work the first time.

	M	Tu	W	Th	F	Sa	Su
The STOP Skill (page 68)							
Considering Pros and Cons (page 69)							
TIPP Your Body Chemistry (page 71)							
Using Temperature (page 72)							
Using Intense Exercise (page 73)							
Pace Your Breathing (page 74)							
Paired Muscle Relaxation (page 75)							
Distract Yourself Using ACCEPTS (page 76)							
Putting ACCEPTS into Action (page 78)							
Self-Soothe with Your Senses (page 79)							
IMPROVE the Moment (page 80)							
Putting IMPROVE into Action (page 81)							
Noticing Nonacceptance (page 84)							
Turn the Mind (page 85)							
Willingness and Willfulness (page 86)							

KEY TAKEAWAYS

We have covered a huge amount in this chapter. You've learned ways to get through bad situations without making things worse and you've learned how accepting pain can reduce suffering. As we move forward, it can be helpful to keep in mind:

- Subjective units of distress (SUDs) can give you helpful clues about what skills to use when.

- Mindfulness skills are all-the-time skills, the core skills of DBT, but come in very handy when distress is especially high. Emotion regulation and interpersonal effectiveness skills are meant to be used when you are experiencing a lower level of distress. The crisis survival skills of distress tolerance are the ones to go to when SUDs are high.

- Assemble crisis survival kits for your home, office, and car and wherever else you may need some assistance in reducing your SUDs.

- Radical acceptance is a very hard skill for most people. Give yourself an advantage by practicing reality acceptance as often as you can.

I can take charge of my emotions rather than letting them take charge of me.

CHAPTER 5

Understanding and Regulating Difficult Emotions

In this chapter we're going to look at the purpose and function of emotions. The DBT skills of emotion regulation will show you how to reduce your vulnerability to emotions by taking care of your mind and body. You'll also learn how to change emotions when they don't fit the facts of the situation or aren't effective to act upon. Emotions give us all sorts of signals about our environment, our safety, who to trust, who to love. But when we view feelings as facts, we can be misled into thinking and behaving in ways that don't sit well with our values and our long-term goals.

Lulu's Story: Dealing with Emotions

Lulu had become almost phobic of emotions. She'd had so many negative experiences, like being told that her emotions were "over the top," or feeling overwhelmed by emotions and not seeing a way out other than harming herself, that she longed never to have any feelings ever again. And the emotions continued to come hot and heavy, unless she was using substances or doing other things to numb herself.

Lulu often felt so overstimulated by emotions that she even feared positive emotions. Someone once told her that being emotionally sensitive was like being naked in a world made of sandpaper. Boy, did that ring true. Sometimes she would feel caught in a mood for days. She often felt powerless to change a mood once it came along, and isolated herself from others for such long periods of time that she wondered why anyone wanted to be her friend anymore. She was so envious of people who could have a bad experience and bounce back. Why couldn't she?

She mentioned this problem to a friend, who shared that she was taking a DBT class. Her friend showed Lulu handouts about skills that would help her regulate her emotions. Lulu's friend told her that this had allowed her to find a greater calm and reduced her vulnerability to negative emotions. This gave Lulu hope that she could do the same.

▶ What Makes It Challenging to Regulate Emotions?

There are many factors that make it difficult for folks to regulate emotions. Use the lines below to reflect on whether each prompt is a reason why regulating emotions is hard for you. Then, write in a journal or other format in more detail about the role each of these factors plays in your emotional life.

Emotional overload: When emotional sensitivity is present, it can be easy to become flooded by emotions and not be able to see how to manage them. What does emotional overload feel like to you?

Lack of skill: Many of us weren't taught how to regulate our emotions; we lacked effective modeling from our caregivers. Is this true for you? How so?

Moodiness: Often, folks have difficulty resisting what their current mood is telling them to do and find it hard to listen to wise mind's urgings. How do your moods affect your decision-making?

Reinforcement of emotional behavior: For some folks, our environment reinforces our emotional behavior. For example, maybe those around us only pay attention when our mood's out of control. How does your environment affect your emotional behavior?

Emotion myths: Myths we hold about emotions can get in the way. For example, believing that feeling emotions makes us bad or weak may keep us from opening up. Do you think you have any myths about emotions?

EMOTIONAL MYTHS

Myths about emotions can often get in the way of being effective in regulating emotions. Challenging these myths helps us choose skills and behaviors that help us reach our goals. Here are some myths about emotions that many people hold, along with some challenges to these myths. Write down your own challenges to these myths in the final column.

Emotion Myth	Challenge to the Myth	My Challenge to the Myth
It's wrong or fake to try to change my emotions.	I can honor and pay attention to my emotions even while I try to regulate them.	I've had times where I deliberately changed my mood and it didn't feel fake.
My emotions should always be trusted; they are who I am.	I can pay attention to my emotions while balancing them with wise mind, which is who I actually am.	
It's important to ignore painful emotions and just be positive.	Ignoring negative emotions can create more pain. Ignoring or suppressing emotions doesn't help me feel better in the long run.	
If others don't understand how I feel, then my feelings must be wrong.	I am allowed to feel however I feel. Others are allowed to feel however they feel.	
If I am emotional, it means I am out of control.	I can have feelings and still make choices that are in line with my goals and values.	

NAMES FOR FEELINGS

Being able to identify feelings starts with increasing your emotional vocabulary. This chart offers a number of descriptive words that you can choose to describe the emotion or emotions you are feeling. Review the list and circle the ones that are most familiar to you. Then keep the list with you and check off the emotions that arise for you over the course of a day (or reflect on this at the end of the day). You aren't limited by the words in the chart, so if you feel something that isn't listed, add it.

Amused	Discouraged	Irritated	Secure
Angry	Embarrassed	Jealous	Selfish
Anxious	Excited	Joyful	Serene
Apathetic	Foolish	Lonely	Thankful
Appreciated	Frustrated	Loving	Thoughtful
Ashamed	Furious	Nurturing	Trusting
Bored	Guilty	Peaceful	Weak
Cheerful	Helpless	Playful	Worthwhile
Confident	Hopeful	Powerful	....
Confused	Hostile	Proud	....
Content	Hurt	Rageful	....
Creative	Important	Rejected	....
Critical	Inadequate	Relaxed	....
Daring	Insecure	Respected	....
Delighted	Insignificant	Sad	....
Depressed	Intelligent	Satisfied	....

HOW WE EXPERIENCE EMOTIONS

These are the five basic experiences we have relating to emotions:

1. **Prompting event:** This is the incident that sets off the emotional experience in the first place. It's something that occurs right before an emotion starts. Some people call these "triggers." They can be external (something that happens outside of you) or internal (your own thoughts or behaviors).

2. **Thoughts:** What you are thinking as you experience an emotion: "I'm the worst." "I can't stand this." "This is so great!"

3. **Feelings:** These are the common names or labels we give to our emotions (sadness, joy, anger).

4. **Body sensations:** How your body responds (tension, butterflies in the stomach, clenched teeth).

5. **Action urges:** Impulses spurred by the emotion (to punch someone in the nose, to run away, to give someone a big hug, to step on someone's cupcake).

Use the following table to record how you experience different emotions in your daily life, to start increasing your awareness of them. You can fill this out after you experience an intense emotion or at the end of your day you can take some time to reflect on the strongest emotion you experienced. The more you do this, the easier it will become, so don't limit yourself to one table; create more blanks to fill in with a separate journal.

The emotion	
Prompting event	
Thoughts	
Feelings	
Body sensations	
Action urges	

▶ Check the Facts

Often we react immediately and automatically to a situation or someone else's behavior. The result: an emotional response. To refocus an emotional response, you can ask yourself these questions to check whether that response is justified by the situation. You may find your emotion or its intensity changing as you answer.

   Try answering these prompts regarding a recent emotional response that didn't go well.

What is the emotion I feel that I want to change?

SUDs before doing this exercise ....

Describe the situation that brought about this emotion using facts only. No judgments!

What are your assumptions and interpretations about the situation? Would someone completely impartial agree with your interpretations?

Are you assuming a threat to your life, your way of life, or your livelihood? What is that threat? How likely is it really to occur? What else could happen?

Is this a catastrophe? If it is (when you really think about it, it almost never is), imagine the catastrophe occurring and you coping well with it. Who could you go to for help?

Was this exercise helpful? What are your SUDs now? ....

OPPOSITE ACTION

When you experience an emotion, it is accompanied by an associated action urge. This is biologically hardwired. There is no morality about it; it's simply a human response. For example:

- When we are angry, we have the urge to verbally or physically attack.

- When we are sad, we have the urge to withdraw and isolate.

- When we are afraid, we have the urge to run from what frightens us.

- When we feel shame, we have the urge to hide away under a rock somewhere.

The problem is that acting on these urges is often not effective in our day-to-day lives. Lashing out? Running away? Not always good strategies for achieving our goals. You may have noticed—and research backs this up—that when we give in to those action urges, we reinforce painful emotions. As a result, we often end up feeling even worse.

Acting *opposite* to an emotion's action urge can be helpful in reducing the intensity of strong feelings. It's difficult to do, but it can help you reroute your negative emotions. This can mean getting active when you feel sad, or gently avoiding (or maybe even being a tiny bit nice to) those with whom you are angry. It can mean approaching scary situations or even owning your mistake when you feel ashamed.

The next time you have an action urge resulting from an intensely emotional state, fill out the worksheet on the next page to get some practice embracing the opposite action. Review the examples for a heads-up on how this technique works. When you are finished, you can re-create this chart elsewhere to keep recording your practice of the technique in the future.

	Example	Your Entries
Emotion	*Fear*	
Situation	*I have been wanting to ask my boss for a raise, but I am afraid he will tell me I don't deserve one.*	
Urge associated with the emotion	*I want to avoid asking for the raise. But, I also have been working really hard and feel like I really deserve one.*	
Opposite action	*I am going to go ahead and ask. I have skills to manage my emotions if he tells me no. I am going to schedule that meeting.*	
How I feel after doing the opposite action	*I feel less afraid. I have made a plan for what to do if he says no, and I am confident that I can handle it.*	

▶ Ideas for Opposite Action

Sometimes you may not be sure what the opposite action is for the emotion you are feeling. Here are some suggestions. Use the space provided to add your own ideas, or expand on the ones that feel like the best fit for you.

Fear: First, ensure the situation is actually safe by checking the facts. If it is, do the thing you are afraid of—over and over until you are no longer afraid. (If the situation is in fact unsafe, see the next exercise, Problem Solving.)

Anger: Take a time-out. Gently avoid the person you are angry with. Be kind to the person you are angry with.

Envy: Make a gratitude list. Resist urges to destroy what the other person has that you do not.

Jealousy: Stop snooping. Let go of controlling the person you fear losing.

Love: Yes, sometimes it is necessary to do opposite action to love. Maybe you are in love with someone who is unavailable, does not treat you well, or is not in love with you. In any of these scenarios, you can avoid that person. Distract yourself when faced with thoughts or memories. Remind yourself why this is not the right person for you to love.

Sadness: Get moving. Do things even though you feel too sad to do them; do things to feel good about yourself.

❭ Problem Solving

Sometimes we can only change an emotion when the problem that is triggering the emotion has been solved. Suppose you feel fear because the lock on your front door is broken and you don't live in a supersafe neighborhood. Your fear is just not going to go away until that lock is fixed, and your landlord is notoriously slow about fixing things. That's when problem solving comes into play. Here are the steps to follow:

1. **Describe the situation.** The lock on your front door is broken. You feel anxious that someone will come into your apartment when you are there and hurt you. The landlord says he will fix it in a few days.

2. **Check the facts.** Anxiety is appropriate for the situation. It is scary to think that someone could enter your home at any time.

3. **Identify your goal.** In this case, to feel safe in your home and not necessarily have to pay the cash for a locksmith yourself.

4. **Brainstorm for solutions.** Offer to the landlord that you will schedule the locksmith so he doesn't have to, and ask the landlord to reimburse you for the cost out of your next rent payment. Get a super big dog to protect you. Go stay somewhere else until the lock is fixed. Ask a friend to stay with you.

5. **Choose a solution.** Because you really want the lock fixed right away, you decide to contact your landlord.

6. **Try your solution.** Your landlord is willing to go with your idea of scheduling the locksmith yourself and reimbursing you by reducing your next rent payment.

7. **Evaluate the results.** Looks like it worked. If the landlord doesn't agree to your proposal, you can go back to step 5 and choose another solution. Then, go through steps 6 and 7. Keep trying solutions until you find one that works.

◗ The Pleasant Activities List

Have you ever noticed that when you are having fun, working toward goals, and taking care of your mind and body you are less likely to be rocked by events that bring about negative emotions?

Positive activities are important for emotional health; they help us build resilience against negative emotions. One caveat, though: It is important to participate mindfully in the activities you choose. It is not enough to mindlessly Netflix your time away. That said, it's okay to watch a TV show you like, so long as it is engaging and you are aware of experiencing it fully and completely.

Positive activities can be big or small. For this practice, try doing a positive activity at least once a day for the following week, especially when you are feeling depleted by demands or overwhelmed with emotions. Evaluate the results and decide how many positive activities you want to plan every week going forward. Here's a list of ideas to start with; add your own to the list.

Bake a cake

Call a friend

Dance

Do a puzzle

Go for a hike

Go out to eat

Go thrifting

Listen to music

Make a to-do list

Organize an area of your home

Pet your pet

Plan a vacation

Play a musical instrument

Read a book

Save money

Sing along to a song

Sip a cup of tea

Take a walk

Think about events you're looking forward to

Try a new hobby

Watch a movie

Watch a sporting event

Other: _____

Other: _____

Other: _____

Other: _____

LIVE ACCORDING TO YOUR VALUES

Small, daily pleasant activities can improve your mood, but they may not help you build the life you want. To accumulate positive emotions in the long term, it is important to identify your values in order to create goals that build toward your life worth living. In this exercise you will be identifying values.

Take a few deep breaths and access your wise mind. Look carefully at the following list of values and circle those that are important to you. These should be values you truly cherish. Don't choose values just because they sound good or are important to your loved ones, your classmates, or your culture. Circle *your* values. Use the extra spaces to add and circle any that aren't included on the list.

Acceptance	Curiosity	Mindfulness
Adventure	Fairness	Persistence
Ambition	Flexibility	Respect
Assertiveness	Forgiveness	Responsibility
Authenticity	Friendliness	Support
Belonging	Fun	Trust
Compassion	Gratitude	Other:_____
Competition	Happiness	Other:_____
Connection	Honesty	Other:_____
Cooperation	Independence	Other:_____
Courage	Kindness	
Creativity	Love	

Which three of the values you circled are most important to you?

Now, narrow that down to just one. Use the space below to reflect on why that value is especially meaningful to you.

FROM A VALUE TO A GOAL

Once you have figured out your most important value, the next step is to decide on specific actions you can take to align your life more closely with this value. In this exercise you'll develop a goal, and then you can figure out the action steps needed to achieve the goal and live according to this value. Review the example, then take your turn!

	Example	My Value
The value	*Connection*	
Three possible goals	*Make new friends.* *Spend more time with loved ones.* *Be more present with my child.*	
Pick one goal	*Make new friends.*	
Three action steps that can move me closer to the goal	*Invite coworkers out for coffee or lunch.* *Look on the internet for meetups I might be interested in.* *Consider volunteering to meet new people.*	
Pick one action step and do it!	*Invite a coworker out for coffee.*	

BUILDING MASTERY

Feeling competent and accomplished makes you feel better. When we do activities that make us feel like we've "got this," we feel confident and capable. That's what we are looking for in the skill of building mastery. This skill is all about choosing to do at least one thing per day, big or small, to feel accomplished and productive. Plan for success in your venture, not failure. Choose something that's challenging but not impossible. For example, if you have never run for exercise before, don't plan to run three miles on your first day. Gradually increase difficulty over time; small progress is still progress. If you aren't feeling challenged, boost the difficulty a bit.

For this exercise, challenge yourself with some activities you'd like to build mastery of. Use the chart to list the challenges on the left, and in the right column, list small daily tasks you can execute to move closer to mastery. An example is provided to guide you.

Challenge	Daily Tasks
Learn to bake a loaf of bread	*Look up articles about bread baking, look up recipes, purchase ingredients, purchase or borrow pan or other tools.*

◗ Cope Ahead for Difficult Situations

Often we have one of two responses in advance of a stress-provoking situation. One is to avoid thinking about the situation at all. The other is to ruminate about all the horrible things that could happen in that particular situation.

The "cope-ahead" skill involves rehearsing ahead of time, so you are prepared to cope skillfully with emotional situations. Here's how to cope ahead, step by step:

1. Describe the situation likely to prompt uncomfortable emotions. Check the facts. Be specific in describing the situation. Name the emotions and actions likely to interfere with using your skills.

2. Decide what skills you want to use in the situation. Be very specific. Write in detail about how you will cope with the situation and with your emotions and action urges.

3. Imagine the situation in your mind as vividly as possible. Then, imagine yourself in the situation, coping well. What skills are you using?

4. What self-soothing or related technique can you use to regulate any emotions that come up as you're using the cope-ahead skill?

❭ Take Care of the Body to Take Care of the Mind

Taking care of your body helps take care of your mind, which is good news when it comes to regulating emotions. The **PLEASE** skill can help you remember to do this. Here's what the acronym stands for:

Physical illness. See a doctor when needed, and take your prescribed medications.

Eating. Eat regularly throughout the day, and eat neither too much nor too little for your needs.

Avoid mood-altering drugs. Keep away from alcohol (or use with moderation), and do not take nonprescribed drugs. Keep an eye on the amount of caffeine you take in and how it impacts you.

Sleep. Get enough sleep and stick to a consistent sleep schedule.

Exercise. Do some sort of physical movement every day.

It can be helpful to review each category in PLEASE and notice if there are changes you can make to improve your physical well-being in order to reduce your emotional vulnerability. For this practice, set a goal to put any changes in place during the coming month.

❯ Drop the Rope

Sometimes we fight our emotions. It can feel like an endless game of tug-of-war, back and forth, trying to make the emotion go away. We pull our end of the rope with all of our might in order to avoid being dragged into the deep, scary pit. But there is an alternative: Stop that tug-of-war with the emotion. Drop the rope. The phrase "dropping the rope" means both stopping the useless fighting, and accepting the feeling.

In other words, dropping the rope and letting the feeling happen, without telling ourselves this emotion will never end or reliving other experiences when we have had this emotion. The idea is to feel this particular emotion, at this time, right now. It helps us to experience that emotions are not catastrophic, that we can be less controlled by emotions and accept our painful emotions as part of the human condition.

To try this out, bring to mind an emotion you would like to stop struggling with. Rate the level of intensity of the feeling on the SUDs scale and record it here: _____. Then, follow these steps:

1. Step back and notice the feeling.

2. Let go of judgments about the feeling.

3. Notice your body sensations.

4. Practice being willing to accept the unwanted feeling.

5. Imagine your feeling is on the car of a train, just passing by.

6. Notice any action urges you might have, without acting on them.

7. Remind yourself of times when you weren't feeling this feeling.

8. Practice completely accepting the feeling.

After you have taken these steps, rate the level of intensity of the feeling again, and record it here: _____. What did you notice about this experience? If you find that you are becoming more distraught during this exercise, move back to crisis survival skills and try again another time.

EMOTION REGULATION DIARY CARD

Using emotion regulation skills on a daily basis will help you not only reduce your baseline level of negative emotion but also help you become more adept at feeling and/or changing negative emotions. Emotion regulation skills are largely change-oriented, and they are vital for moving toward your life worth living. Set a goal to practice one or more emotion regulation skills each day in the coming week. Use the following scale to rate how well each skill helped regulate your emotions and record the number on the day of the week you tried it. Rating: 1 = Didn't help at all; 2 = Helped a little; and 3 = Helped a lot.

Remember to keep trying the skills to gain mastery with them. Some skills may never be easy, but can still make a huge difference in your life.

	M	Tu	W	Th	F	Sa	Su
How We Experience Emotions (page 98)							
Check the Facts (page 99)							
Opposite Action (page 100)							
Problem Solving (page 103)							
From a Value to a Goal (page 106)							
Building Mastery (page 107)							
Cope Ahead for Difficult Situations (page 108)							
Take Care of the Body to Take Care of the Mind (page 109)							
Drop the Rope (page 110)							

In this chapter, you've learned all about emotion regulation. You've gained insight into how to reduce vulnerability to negative emotions. You've seen how checking the facts and using opposite action can change your emotions. You've also learned that using mindfulness to experience an emotion can keep it from becoming overwhelming. As we move along, it may be helpful to keep in mind:

- Please use the PLEASE skill. When we are sick, not eating or sleeping well, or taking drugs that aren't prescribed to us, we are particularly prone to all kinds of negative emotions.

- When experiencing an emotion that may not fit the facts of the situation or is too intense or long-lasting, opposite action can help.

- Don't underplay the importance of mindfully participating in pleasant events. Everyone needs positive events in their lives to be happy.

- Use your values to determine your goals, and work toward these goals in order to create your life worth living.

*I can communicate my
needs and wants in ways
that help me maintain
my relationships and
my self-respect.*

CHAPTER 6

Respecting Yourself and Others with Interpersonal Effectiveness

This chapter is devoted to the final DBT module of interpersonal effectiveness: building and keeping relationships in your life. We'll take a look at what gets in the way of being interpersonally effective. After that, you'll learn how to balance your emphasis in your communications. You'll see how the DEAR MAN skill can help you get what you want in an interaction. You'll discover how to improve your relationships with validation and the GIVE skill. You'll learn how to maintain your self-respect using the FAST skill. We'll also focus on relational mindfulness, finding and keeping friends, and ending destructive relationships. I think you'll be excited at the potential changes these skills can bring to your life, so let's go!

Stefan's Story: Navigating Relationships

Stefan just wasn't sure he was built to be with other people. It seemed like his relationships started off great; he met new people he clicked with and in no time he felt very close to them. But sometimes he was so afraid they wouldn't like him anymore that he would do whatever they wanted. And he'd end up feeling like he had lost himself and resentful that he never seemed to get his way.

So he would end that relationship either by blowing it up because he was angry that they didn't seem to care what he really wanted, or by ghosting them because he was too fearful to make his needs known. Or the other person would end the relationship because they felt like he was "too clingy" or his emotions were "too much." Even with his family, who he knew loved him, Stefan would become angry or distraught if he thought they were judging him or didn't understand his emotions.

Stefan started to do some research and saw that skills for relationship improvement were included in DBT. Up until then, Stefan didn't know that he could learn how to manage his emotions and improve his ability to communicate with others. He tried a few of the skills he learned about online. He felt a little awkward and uncomfortable at first, but as he kept using them he started to see a difference in how others interacted with him.

◗ What Is Interpersonal Effectiveness?

When it comes to interpersonal effectiveness, the goal is to ask for what you want and be able to say no, all while maintaining your relationships and self-respect. These skills help with figuring out what you want and getting others to take your opinions seriously, as well as building and strengthening relationships. They also help us deal with conflicts and problems as they arise rather than letting resentments build up until relationships end.

Some people who learn these skills write them off and say they don't work. Why? They try them once or twice and don't get what they want. It's important to understand that there's no guarantee that these skills will automatically make others do what we want or stop doing things we dislike. Sometimes people just want to do what they want to do. Sometimes what we want doesn't seem reasonable or possible to someone else. There are lots of obstacles to interpersonal effectiveness, but that's true for both those who know DBT skills and those who don't. Please learn these skills and practice them frequently. Although you will not always get what you want, you will benefit from more success in your relationships.

First, let's explore what gets in the way of interpersonal effectiveness in your current relationships. Read about the following barriers, and record your experience of how they've been present in your life or how you've been successful in overcoming them.

Lacking skills. When you're short on skills in interpersonal situations, you may not know what to say or how to act when communicating with others. This isn't cause for self-blame. We don't always get the chance to learn from role models how to handle social situations, or we don't get to practice certain social behaviors.

Not knowing what you want. Maybe you know what to say, what to do, or how to act. But you don't know what you want from your interactions. Communication becomes confusing when you are unclear about what you want or what you're trying to accomplish. And you may not know when to ask for your needs to be met or when to say no to others' requests.

Continued on next page ➤

Emotional barriers. The skills are there, but your emotions get in your way. Behaviors can be mood-dependent when emotion mind is in charge. Our emotions take over and we do what we feel. We say things that can't be taken back, no matter who or what gets in the way. Or we don't speak up when we should.

Sacrificing long-term goals for short-term goals. You may feel strong urges to avoid or stop an emotion, no matter the long-term consequences. Say you hate feeling anxious, so you avoid social situations. Short-term avoidance reduces that anxiety. But you also feel lonely. Making friends is the only thing that will reduce loneliness in the long term. That requires socializing to meet potential friends, even if it makes you anxious in the short term.

Interference from other people. Asking for what you want in the most effective way may not be enough if you're asking someone more powerful than you. Unfortunately, that's how it is. No matter how compelling your arguments are, the police officer can still issue a ticket. Your boss can decline your raise request for any number of reasons. It's just out of your hands sometimes.

Belief system barriers. When you hold beliefs that impede communication, even the best skills won't help. Some people fear that if they ask for what they want, or say no to a request, others will be angry or judge them. Some believe other people should know what they want without having to be told, which certainly hinders effective communication. Some people believe that asking for help indicates weakness. Beliefs like these make it hard to be effective interpersonally. Here's some help overcoming this barrier: Check your facts.

Myths about communication can get in the way of being effective in inter-personal situations. Challenging these myths can help us choose skills and behaviors that help us obtain our goals. Here are some common myths about communication, along with some challenges to those myths. Review and write in your personal challenges to these myths.

Communication Myth	Challenge to the Myth	My Challenge to the Myth
People who care about me should know what I need.	It is vital to communicate to others; they cannot read my mind.	
Other people should always like or approve of me.	Some folks just aren't going to like me or approve of everything I do. I don't like or approve of everyone, either.	
Saying no is selfish and mean.	Everyone has needs. I am allowed to look out for mine.	
Asking for what I want is pushy and self-centered.	Asking for what I want is important to getting my needs met.	
It is weak to ask for help.	All humans need help sometimes.	
I shouldn't be fair or respectful to others if they aren't fair and respectful to me.	I can act in accordance with my values of treating others with fairness and respect no matter how they treat me.	

CLARIFYING YOUR PRIORITIES

There are three factors to consider when preparing for an interaction in which you want your needs met: getting what we want, maintaining the relationships, and maintaining our self-respect. We generally wish to achieve all three, but the importance of each depends on the situation. For instance, if you are speaking with a customer service representative, you might prioritize getting what you want. If you are interacting with someone who is important to you, all three factors could be equally important.

Let's explore what's important to you when it comes to each priority. Choose an interaction that includes a need you want met. It could be a recent scenario or an interaction you're expecting in the near future. Apply the following questions.

Getting what you want. When it comes to getting what you want, what is important to you in this interaction? Rank the statements below, choosing the most, second most, and least important.

☐ Having my needs met.

☐ Resolving a disagreement.

☐ Being heard, having my point taken seriously.

Questions to ask yourself: What do I want from this interaction? What will be the best strategy to obtain this?

....

....

....

....

....

....

Keeping the relationship solid (or even improving it). What is important to you regarding your relationship to the other person? Check the statements that apply.

☐ Behaving in a way that the other person will still like me.

☐ Taking care of the relationship.

☐ Balancing my short-term needs with the longer-term health of the relationship.

Questions to ask yourself: How do I want this person to feel about me after this interaction is over? What is the best strategy to achieve this goal?

....

....

Keeping your self-respect. How important is your self-respect to this interaction? Check the statements that are important to you when it comes to keeping your self-respect.

☐ Behaving in a way that aligns with my values.

☐ Being fair to the other person, but also to myself.

☐ Being capable and competent, not acting helpless when I am not.

Questions to ask yourself: How do I want to feel about myself after this interaction is completed? What strategies do I need to use to feel that way about me?

....

....

◗ Asking for What You Want with DEAR MAN

DEAR MAN is a way to structure conversations to make it more likely that you get what you want. Remember, sometimes you can be as skillful as you possibly can be and the thing you are looking for just may not be available. Despite this caveat, DEAR MAN is a powerful tool for improving communication. You can think of the DEAR portion as the script for what you want to say in the interaction, and MAN as how to deliver your message. Let's start with an explanation and example of the script.

Describe the facts of the situation. Keep judgments out of it. Putting the facts forward will get you and the other person on the same page, with a few specifics that you can both agree upon. For example, your boss, Steve, often asks you to stay late with little notice. You would really like at least twenty-four hours' warning. First, you describe the situation: "Steve, you've asked me to stay late three times this week close to the end of the day."

Express your feelings about the situation. Don't expect the other person to read your mind; help them understand your point of view. Be brief and don't get lost in your feelings. Example: "I really like working here, but it's hard for me to plan my life when you ask me to work late with only an hour of notice."

Assert yourself by asking for what you want (which might mean saying "no" in certain situations). Don't be vague or expect others to guess what you want. Clarity is key. Example: "I would really appreciate it if you could tell me the day prior when you want me to stay late to work on something."

Reinforce yourself by explaining to the other person how it will benefit them to do what you want them to do. Example: "It would be better for our working relationship if I had more notice. You may have noticed that sometimes I can get a bit frazzled or snappy when things are very last-minute. I am so much more upbeat and more productive when I know what's coming."

Now, we know what we should say, here's how to say it:

Mindful. Staying mindful means not getting distracted by the other person's attempts to change the subject or make verbal attacks. Be prepared to simply repeat your request. Example: It might be hard for Steve to hear that I have been unhappy, and he may be defensive. I will make sure to stay mindful of my goal and not get pulled into a wider discussion.

Appear confident. Even if you don't feel confident, fake it. Acting more confident can help you feel more confident. Check that your posture, tone of voice, and eye contact help you convey your message. Example: When I speak, I'll make sure that my posture is upright, my tone is gentle but forthright, and that I make eye contact, even if I feel nervous.

Negotiate. Be willing to negotiate and be prepared with different solutions. Offer to solve the problem in different ways. Example: "If Steve is resisting, I could offer to keep one day a week flexible for late hours."

For this practice, study the DEAR MAN strategy and try it in a low-stakes interaction, just to get a feel for how it works. We'll take a more detailed look in the next exercise.

CRAFTING YOUR DEAR MAN

Before you head into a conversation that matters, write out a **DEAR** script and jot down a few notes and encouraging statements for **MAN**.

Describe. Describe the current situation to the other person, using facts only.

....

Express. Express how you feel about the situation.

....

Assert. Ask for what you want or say no. Don't assume the other person knows what you want. How will you phrase your assertion?

....

Reinforce. Explain to the other person what's in it for them. What is their benefit for giving you what you want?

....

Mindful. Don't get distracted by the other person trying to change the subject or making verbal attacks. Just keep repeating your request or saying no. What's the main need you're trying to meet?

....

Appear confident. Even if you don't feel confident, fake it. You have a right to ask, even if the other person says no. What can you do to project confidence?

....

Negotiate. Be willing to negotiate and come up with different solutions. What are some alternatives you're willing to consider?

....

◗ Validation to Improve Relationships

Do you recall a time when you were really emotional and talked to someone who completely understood what you were feeling? Did you notice that the tension in your body started to melt away and your emotions became less intense? That's the power of validation! But what is it? Validation means you listen to someone with an accepting and open mind and communicate your understanding of their emotions and experiences back to them. Validation is attained not when you get it but when the other person gets that you get it. Here's how you do it:

Pay attention. Give the other person your full attention, in ways they'll recognize. Make eye contact, listen actively (nod, lean in, react appropriately), and show with your facial expressions that you are not judging.

Reflect back. Make sure you understand what the other person said by reflecting back what you heard. You don't have to repeat it exactly, just paraphrase it. Let yourself feel some of what the other person is feeling.

Ask questions. Don't get too attached to your interpretation of what you're hearing. Make a gentle guess and ask for confirmation. If you aren't right, let it go.

Stand in their shoes. Try to understand how the other person's feelings, behaviors, or thoughts fit with their life struggles, recent challenges, or current state of mind. You can empathize with their feelings even if you disagree with their actions or their facts.

Acknowledge the valid. When facts are correct and behaviors would make sense to anyone, validation becomes easier.

Convey radical genuineness. The definition of radical genuineness is the ability to understand the experience of another as an equal rather than seeing them as a victim or as different than you. The key is to respect and understand someone's experience on a deep level. Be respectful to the person without being patronizing or condescending.

For this practice, study the above principles and look for an opportunity to use them in a conversation with a friend or colleague. You might focus on one or two at first, then add more to your repertoire when you're ready.

▶ Self-Validation to Improve Your Relationship with Yourself

As important as it is to validate others, it is equally important to learn to validate yourself. When you find yourself talking to yourself in an invalidating way, remember the following tips:

Don't judge. Let go of judgments of yourself, especially because judging ourselves often leads to shame, which is just going to increase your level of negative emotion.

Check the facts. Remember to check your facts before validating yourself. It is not helpful to validate facts that are inaccurate. Here's an example: You have a dream that your sweetheart cheated on you. It just wouldn't be effective to validate your belief that your sweetie cheated on you and affirm your instinct to leave that sneaky jerkface, because it was just a dream. But you sure can validate the anxiety, anger, and sadness you may have felt as a result of the dream.

Don't discount your feelings. Your emotional experience is something that is up for validation. Your emotions make sense in light of your life experience, your current situation, and your vulnerabilities.

Be kind. Remember to speak to yourself as if you were a dear friend. You would never speak to a friend with the harshness you use on yourself, right?

▶ Coping with Invalidation

Let's face it, being invalidated sucks. But, as shown in the previous example, invalidation can sometimes be helpful, such as when your facts just aren't true. But invalidation can come in many unhelpful forms, including being ignored, misread, misinterpreted, trivialized, or receiving unequal treatment. Answer these prompts to ease the pain of invalidation:

Think of a time you were invalidated by someone else. What was the situation and what emotions did you feel in response to this invalidation?

Write a validation statement regarding those emotions.

What could you have done to soothe yourself in that situation? Think particularly about the self-soothing skills in distress tolerance (page 79).

Finally, write a self-soothing statement you could say to yourself in the situation.

▶ GIVE to Improve and Maintain Relationships

The **GIVE** skill is all about keeping and maintaining relationships. The question to answer for yourself in preparation for this skill is, "How do I want the other person to feel about me?" This skill is about how you treat the other person while you deliver your DEAR MAN, or how you interact with other folks in general. A benefit of being nice to people is that they are more likely to give us what we want. Secondly, kinder, more compassionate treatment of others generally makes us feel better about ourselves.

(Be) Gentle. Remember that you might actually care about this relationship, this person, this human. Be nice. No attacks or threats. Steer clear of judgments. Stick to the facts and stay gentle in your approach.

(Act) Interested. Take the time to listen to the other person. Sometimes you'll have to keep listening to someone long after they've gotten their point across. Or you'll have to hear them talk about something that's not important to you. That's why the skill is to (act) interested, not to (be) interested.

Validate. Keep in mind the validation skills you learned earlier in this chapter (page 125). Here's another idea: functional validation, showing someone with your actions that you take them seriously. If someone is crying, hand them a tissue. If someone says they need space, give them some time alone. We can all talk the talk. Functional validation is about walking the walk.

Easy manner. Try to be lighthearted and maybe even a little humorous if it is appropriate. Try to make the situation more comfortable even if it's serious and intense. More often, I find that when people speak as if the entire world is about to end, in reality life will go on after even the most difficult interactions. Even the smallest acknowledgment of that—maybe using a pet name with a loved one or avoiding the "we need to talk" tone of voice—can help.

❯ Putting GIVE into Action

Think of a situation during which it would have been helpful to use the **GIVE** skill. Answer these prompts to further explore using GIVE.

Briefly describe the situation: ....

....

(Be) Gentle. How would you have been gentler in this interaction?

....

....

(Act) Interested. How would you have acted interested in this situation?

....

....

Validate. How would you have been more validating in this situation?

....

....

Easy manner. How would you have shown more of an easy manner in this situation?

....

....

How well did the conversation go? Consider how using GIVE would alter the outcome of this situation and how it would result in differences within your relationship.

▶ Maintaining Self-Respect with FAST

The FAST skill is intended to be used when you need to make sure you walk away from an interaction feeling like you behaved with integrity and that you maintained your self-respect. How do you want to feel about yourself? That's the question you are answering here. Was I fair and true to my values, or did I use threats or lies to get what I wanted? Here's what the **FAST** skill contains:

Fair. It is important to be fair not only to yourself but also to the other person. Taking advantage of others makes it difficult to respect yourself. Conversely, giving in to others and not standing up for yourself can make you disrespect yourself as well. Maintaining your self-respect is easier when you try to be fair.

(No) Apologies. This doesn't mean never apologize. It's only natural to apologize if you've made a mistake. But it's not good to apologize for living, for breathing, for having needs, for taking up space, for asking for anything, or for saying no. You have a right to ask for things and to say no. Also, constantly apologizing can be pretty annoying to others and can negatively impact relationships. So can constantly asking others if they are mad at you, so avoid that, too.

Stick to your values. Try not to give up your values or opinions in order to keep someone's favor. It's difficult to hold your own values when you think others are judging you for your beliefs, or you feel you don't necessarily have a right to your own beliefs.

Truthful. Try to develop a pattern of honesty in your relationships. Don't act helpless when you are not, and work toward mastery rather than trying to get others to take care of things for you. Try not to exaggerate or make up excuses.

▶ Putting FAST into Action

Now, let's practice putting FAST into action. Think of a situation when it would have been helpful to use the FAST skill. Briefly describe the circumstances:

Now answer these prompts to further explore using the **FAST** skill.

Fair. How would you have been more fair in this interaction?

(No) Apologies. How would you have apologized less in this situation?

Stick to your values. How would you have stuck to your values in this situation?

Truthful. How would you have been more truthful in this situation?

Spend a moment to consider how you think using the FAST skill would have altered the outcome of this situation and how you think it would have resulted in changes to your self-respect.

▶ Relational Mindfulness

Often, when interacting with other people, we are so focused on how we think and feel that we aren't mindful enough of others. Increasing your relational mindfulness improves your relationships and makes them last longer. Applying the mindfulness skills can be really helpful in increasing our relational mindfulness.

Here are some tips to practice it yourself:

- Pay attention to others with curiosity and interest; let go of self-consciousness or a focus on self.

- Focus on what they are saying rather than planning what you will say next.

- Observe your judgments and let them go.

- Focus on thinking dialectically. Ask yourself, "What can I learn from this person?" rather than thinking, "What are they saying that is wrong?"

- Give others the benefit of the doubt. Don't automatically assume negative motives or what they think of you.

- Throw yourself into interactions; become one with activities and conversations.

- Go with the flow rather than trying to be in charge.

- Oh, and no multitasking. Put down that phone!

PRACTICING RELATIONAL MINDFULNESS

The next time you practice relational mindfulness, review this list afterward and check off the skills you used.

☐ Paid attention with curiosity and interest.

☐ Let go of self-consciousness and/or focus on self.

☐ Focused on what they were saying rather than what I would say next.

☐ Observed my judgments and let them go.

☐ Used dialectical thinking.

☐ Gave others the benefit of the doubt.

☐ Threw myself into the conversation/activity.

☐ Went with the flow, didn't try to control the situation.

☐ Didn't multitask.

Now, answer these questions. First, who were you with?

How did you feel during the interaction?

How did you feel afterward?

Did you see a difference in how being mindful affected your interaction with this person?

INTERPERSONAL EFFECTIVENESS DIARY CARD

Using interpersonal effectiveness skills regularly is a big part of getting what you want, improving your relationships, and maintaining your self-respect. Set a goal to try out one more of the skills in this chapter each day in the coming week. Use the following scale to rate the effectiveness of each skill and record the number on the day of the week you tried it. Rating: 1 = Didn't help at all; 2 = Helped a little; 3 = Helped a lot.

Remember, it may take some practice for skills to be truly effective. Sometimes the environment will be too powerful, or people just won't be able or willing to honor your requests. In any case, continuing to be interpersonally effective will build your sense of mastery and self-respect.

	M	Tu	W	Th	F	Sa	Su
Clarifying Your Priorities (page 120)							
Asking for What You Want with DEAR MAN (page 122)							
Crafting Your DEAR MAN (page 124)							
Validation to Improve Relationships (page 125)							
Self-Validation to Improve Your Relationship with Yourself (page 126)							
Coping with Invalidation (page 127)							
Putting GIVE into Action (page 129)							
Putting FAST into Action (page 131)							
Practicing Relational Mindfulness (page 133)							

KEY TAKEAWAYS

We've covered a lot of ways to communicate in this chapter. We've focused on how to interact in ways that build self-respect and improve relationships. You've learned how to make it more likely you will have your requests honored. We've talked about what gets in the way of benign, effective ways to find new friendships and end destructive relationships. As you continue to improve your skills, it may be helpful to keep in mind:

- Be clear about your goals before you enter into significant communication. Ask yourself: What do I want? How do I want the other person to feel about me? How do I want to feel about myself?

- When planning a DEAR MAN, create a script to help you think carefully about what you will say and how you would like to say it.

- Validation is communication magic. When someone understands that you understand and accept their experience, it enhances relationships and builds trust. Remember to validate yourself!

- Focusing on relational mindfulness can improve your relationships and make them last longer.

I am working toward my goals and building a life that is worth living.

CHAPTER 7

Strategies for Maintaining Progress

We've spent the last four chapters learning the DBT modules: mindfulness, distress tolerance, emotion regulation, and interpersonal effectiveness. In this final chapter, you'll find tools to track your progress, emotions, and behaviors. They will help you make lasting changes that will move you toward your life worth living. Increasing your ability to regulate emotions is not a linear process. You will experience ups and downs as you work to develop and adopt new ways of dealing with difficult situations and emotions. The tools in this chapter will help you stay motivated and on track toward meeting your goals.

Renata's Story: Finding Her Life Worth Living

When Renata was diagnosed with BPD, she was taken aback. She had heard about the diagnosis and knew there was a lot of stigma around it. On the other hand, she was relieved to know there was a name for what she was coping with.

She had read that DBT was a treatment that was supposed to be effective, but she'd been in therapy before and hadn't had the best experience. Still, Renata wanted to learn how to better manage her symptoms, so she read up about DBT and decided she would give it her best try.

Although she felt a bit overwhelmed, she decided to fully commit herself to becoming as skillful as possible. She joined a Facebook group of people who were in DBT treatment or who were trying to apply DBT on their own. She was surprised at how supportive the community was and how they were able to give helpful suggestions. She was inspired and encouraged by their success and felt validated by their struggles.

Renata set aside time each day to do her diary card and regularly followed behavioral chain analysis to better understand her problem behaviors. Bit by bit, she saw progress; situations that once would have been impossible to get through seemed more manageable. Her partner seems calmer, less on edge, and more ready to discuss problems with her rather than avoid them or sweep them under the rug. Over time, Renata found that life became more rewarding and meaningful and that she was much more than her BPD diagnosis.

◗ Reviewing Your Life-Worth-Living Goal

Back in chapter 3, you created a life-worth-living goal (page 37). Hopefully, equipped with all the insight and skills you've gained throughout the course of this workbook, your goal feels much more attainable.

Take some time to reflect on your original goal and use the space provided below to clarify it even further—or replace it, if that's how you feel. Consider now how you would define a life that is meaningful and important to you. Think of your friends, romantic relationships, family, education, work, meaningful pastimes, and how or where you want to live when considering your life worth living.

To help clarify your goal, imagine that you woke up tomorrow, your problems were reduced, and your life was going well—maybe not perfectly, but well. What would make your life worth living? What would your goal be? Be as specific as possible.

What changes do you think need to occur in your life to fully realize your goal? For example: If your ultimate goal is to feel happier, you might write about how your work situation or relationships need to change.

Now, write about what regular behaviors can help you make these changes. For example, regular use of DBT skills to help you cope with strong emotions.

Finally, what behaviors do you need to avoid? These would be the behaviors that get in the way of your life worth living; for example, using substances or engaging in self-harm to cope with strong emotions, or any other behaviors that get in the way of creating the life you want.

Tracking Your Journey with Diary Cards

For folks with big emotional responses, movement toward goals can easily be derailed, with no ill intent on the part of anyone involved. Because things often feel like crises, long-term goals can fall by the wayside, and there is little to no time to learn skills or make strides that lead to a life worth living. Memory plays a role here as well. Sometimes it feels like how you feel today is how it has always been, and it is difficult to remember that yesterday or the day before went well.

Tracking your progress allows you to identify patterns that may be slowing you down, gain insight into your behaviors, and create plans for future situations. It also allows you to see how you've improved over time, which can be especially helpful on the days when you feel discouraged.

How exactly do we track progress? With diary cards. You already have a head start on using these because of the skill cards at the end of chapters 3 to 6. In this chapter, you will find other diary cards, including ones to track the behaviors you are looking to increase or decrease, and a card to track your emotions.

The idea is that you mindfully fill out your diary card(s) on a daily basis. Creating a ritual around filling them out can be really helpful. Some folks take time at the end of the day, prior to bed, to reflect on the day. Others take some time in the morning to reflect on the previous day's events. Setting a timer, or putting the diary card in a place where you will be reminded to complete it, can help you remember. Staying on track with your cards is especially helpful while you are learning and mastering DBT skills. Some people stop using them once they feel they have successfully integrated the skills into their lives, and others continue on a regular basis to help keep them on track toward their goals.

After you finish using the diary cards in earlier chapters and on the following pages, I encourage you to keep recording your experiences outside this book. An internet search for DBT Diary Card will pull up a bunch of diary cards that consolidate this information on a page or two in order to keep all of your information for the week together. I have a link to one I use with instructions for filling it out in the Resources section (page 158). You can also find helpful diary card apps in the app store on your smartphone by searching DBT Diary Card.

RECORDING YOUR EMOTIONS

When you track your emotions, you will become better at identifying them and tying them to events throughout the week. Besides tracking negative emotions, you will also track positive emotions. That helps us see that even in the midst of challenging emotions like anxiety and sadness, joy and happiness can be present, too.

A daily, mindful reflection and recording of your emotions can give you a much better understanding of how, why, and when your emotions fire, which is critical to learning how to regulate them. On a scale of 0 to 5, note the highest intensity of the particular emotion each day. If you find yourself feeling other emotions that it might be helpful to track and explore, add them in the blank spaces provided.

		M	Tu	W	Th	F	Sa	Su
Anxiety	0 to 5							
Sadness	0 to 5							
Shame	0 to 5							
Compassion	0 to 5							
Joy	0 to 5							
Anger	0 to 5							
	0 to 5							
	0 to 5							

TRACKING UNHELPFUL URGES AND BEHAVIORS

In addition to tracking skills use, as you've done in previous chapters, you'll use diary cards to track unhelpful urges and behaviors that you experience over the course of a week, as well as helpful behaviors.

Common unhelpful behaviors to target are suicidal ideation, self-harm behaviors, using alcohol or drugs to numb or avoid emotions, and other unhelpful coping strategies like isolating from others or reacting angrily to others. You'll note that the card tracks your urge to engage in an unhelpful behavior; that means having the thought and desire to do the behavior, though you might not act on it. You'll track urges on a scale of 0 to 5, with 5 being the strongest urge. When you actually engage in the behavior, you will indicate yes or no on the diary card.

You'll see that suicidal ideation and self-harm behaviors are listed as target behaviors to decrease. If you don't have those issues, great! They are commonly listed on DBT diary cards because even if you don't regularly deal with those behaviors, it is important to pay attention if urges crop up. Space is provided in the final rows to name other unhelpful behaviors you are targeting.

Here's an example: Let's say you are working on decreasing reacting angrily to your partner. One day you experience moderate urges to snap at your partner, but you use the STOP skill and are able to refrain. You would record a 3 for urges, and "N" for action that day. The next day, your urges feel stronger, and you let your partner have it that day. You record 5 for urges and "Y" for action.

If you are in therapy, it's helpful to share your card with your therapist so that you can both determine the behaviors that need the most attention. If you are working on your own (although I highly recommend an accountability partner, someone else who is also working toward being more skillful), reviewing the card on a weekly basis and doing behavior chain analysis and solution analysis (more about those coming up) around behaviors that get in the way of your life-worth-living goal will likely keep you on track.

There is also a table to track helpful behaviors, which may include engaging in self-care activities, enjoying time with loved ones, or creating a schedule for your day. Think of five that you find most helpful and write these in the rows of the first column. As the week progresses, mark the days you engaged in each behavior.

Unhelpful Behaviors to Decrease		M	Tu	W	Th	F	Sa	Su
Suicidal ideation or actions	Urges (0 to 5)							
	Action (Y/N)							
Self-harm behaviors	Urges (0 to 5)							
	Action (Y/N)							
Other: _____	Urges (0 to 5)							
	Action (Y/N)							
Other: _____	Urges (0 to 5)							
	Action (Y/N)							
Other: _____	Urges (0 to 5)							
	Action (Y/N)							

Helpful Behaviors to Increase	M	Tu	W	Th	F	Sa	Su

Analyzing Behavior

The process of changing a behavior can be challenging, but it's an important focus of DBT. It is especially important to change behaviors that make us feel good in the short term but hinder us in the long run. It can be a bit easier to understand behavior if you understand the drivers behind it.

In DBT, we use a behavior chain analysis to help you understand what function a problem behavior serves and all the factors that contribute to that behavior. You can arrive at that understanding by analyzing all the things that led up to the behavior—looking at how they are connected like the links in a chain. This is the structure of a DBT behavior chain:

Vulnerabilities: These are stressors that made you more prone to the behavior in question, whether they occurred in the twenty-four to forty-eight hours beforehand or they're ongoing issues. Illness, poor eating, poor sleeping, substance use, intense emotions, and stressful events can all make you vulnerable to engaging in problematic behaviors.

Prompting event: This is the occurrence that set off the chain of events that led to the problem behavior. Consider it the straw that broke the camel's back; if this specific event hadn't occurred, the problem behavior probably wouldn't have happened. Prompting events can be internal (thoughts, memories, flashbacks, feelings) or external (things around you, someone saying something).

Links: Links in the chain are the events that came after the prompting event leading to the problem behavior. It is important to pay attention to each link in the chain. Links generally fit into following categories: actions (things you do); body sensations (things you feel in your body); thoughts (including expectations, judgments, etc.); events in the environment (including things others do); and emotions (yours, not those of other people).

Target behavior: This is the behavior you want to change.

Consequences: These are the positives and negatives that come about due to the target behavior.

In a chain analysis, we find out what happened and gain a lot of information about the factors contributing to our problem behavior. Once it's finished, you can move on to a solution analysis, which allows you to brainstorm more effective ways of dealing with a similar situation in the future.

BEHAVIOR CHAIN AND SOLUTION ANALYSIS WORKSHEET

Now it's your turn. Bring to mind a recent incident that resulted in a problem behavior that you would like to change. Fill out the form as completely as you can. Remember, this is not an opportunity to beat yourself up! Please treat yourself with compassion during this process. First, work through the chain of behavior in each row of the left-hand column. Then, in the right-hand column, fill out your solution analysis, noting the DBT skills you might use in a similar situation to help with each part of the behavior chain, along with any other notes.

Chain Analysis	Solution Analysis
Vulnerability factors:	Ways to reduce vulnerability in the future:
Prompting event:	Ways to prevent the prompting event in the future (if possible):
Links:	Different, more skillful behaviors to use to prevent or reverse each link:
Target behavior:	What I'd like to do next time:
Consequences:	Plans to correct or make good (as much as possible) consequences that occurred:

CREATING A SKILLS PLANS FOR THE FUTURE

You've learned how to analyze past behavior in order to plan for different behavior in the future. You can also make plans for enacting future skillful behavior, even if a problem behavior has not yet occurred. First, answer these questions:

Problem behavior I want to avoid:

Behavior I would like to do instead:

Now, fill out the following tables, noting your challenges in the left-hand columns, and the skills you can use to address each challenge in the opposite columns.

Anticipated Vulnerability Factors	How Can I Address These Vulnerabilities?

Anticipated Promoting Events	Can I Avoid This Event? Can I Prepare for These Events?

Unhelpful Thoughts I Might Have	More Effective Thoughts

Crisis Urges I Might Have	Ways to Distract, Self-Soothe, or Improve the Moment

Ineffective Behaviors in which I Might Be Tempted to Engage	Alternative More-Skillful Behaviors

Emotions I Might Have	Ways to Check the Facts, Practice Opposite Action, or Self-Validate

Consequences of Engaging in Crisis Urges or Other Ineffective Behaviors	Benefits of Staying Skillful

PREPARING FOR CRISIS: MAKING A SAFETY PLAN

You know what they say: "Hope for the best, plan for the worst." Let's do that here by creating a safety plan. This is a prioritized written list of coping strategies and sources of support that you can use during a crisis when you are experiencing suicidal ideation or the urge to engage in any other behavior that could endanger you. I truly hope you never need to use it, but it's best to have one anyway. Fill in the prompts below to create your plan.

My Safety Plan

I commit to consulting this document and using the resources listed here if I begin experiencing suicidal ideation, especially if I am planning how to die or if I feel the urge to engage in any other behavior that could endanger me.

Signed: _____

Date: _____

Step 1: Identify the warning signs. What are the thoughts, images, moods, situations, behaviors that signal to me a crisis may be developing?

1. _____

_____

2. _____

_____

3. _____

_____

Step 2: Use internal coping strategies. What are the skills I can use to take my mind off my problems without contacting another person? Review the distress tolerance skills if needed, especially ACCEPTS (page 76), Self-Soothing (page 79), and IMPROVE (page 80).

1. ....

....

2. ....

....

3. ....

....

Step 3: Turn to people and social settings that provide distraction. Write the names and contact info for people you can call or reach out to.

1. ....

....

2. ....

....

3. ....

....

Continued on next page ➤

Step 4: Contact people I can ask for help from. Write down their names and contact numbers.

1. ....

2. ....

3. ....

Step 5: Contact an emergency response professional. I will reach out to one of the following contacts:

1. 911. Local emergency services vary in their response to mental health crises, but if you are in immediate danger and have no other alternative, this may be your best bet. (Consider researching the response protocol in your area.)

2. DontCallthePolice.com has listings of alternatives to calling 911 for mental health emergencies. List resources for your area here:

....

....

....

3. Suicide and Crisis Lifeline: 988 (toll-free)

4. The emergency room of my local hospital:

....

5. Write down the contact details of other emergency response profession-als you may wish to reach out to, such as your physician, therapist, or alternate ERs.

Step 6: Make the environment safe. This means getting rid of, or handing over to someone else, things you can use to harm yourself, including firearms, sharp objects, and medication. Note these items and your plan to rid yourself of them.

Step 7: Reflect on the people and things that are most important to me and worth living for. Write these down to reflect on.

If you experience suicidal ideation or intense urges, please don't take these issues lightly. Seek professional help if you are in danger of harming yourself. This safety plan, and this book, are not substitutes for therapy.

◗ Maintaining Motivation

Staying the course in targeting problem behaviors and increasing skills use is a big commitment. Finding and maintaining motivation is important! Identifying your reasons for doing DBT is vital to finding, keeping, and maintaining your motivation. So remember to go back to your life-worth-living goal often, to provide motivation when yours is flagging. You might, in moments of emotion mind, say, "That goal is impossible" or "I don't care about that goal anymore." Watch out for this. It is true that goals can change, but it is vital that you engage wise mind when deciding to change your life-worth-living goal, not discard it in a moment of high emotion mind.

Be gentle with yourself when your motivation wanes. Sometimes, we just don't have the energy. That's human. Here are some tips for increasing your ability to follow through when motivation is low:

Create the right environment. Make it easier to use skills or follow through on tasks and activities that reduce your vulnerability to emotion mind. For example, if exercise helps you manage stress, pack your exercise bag the night before to make it easier to hit the gym in the morning. If access to certain items increases your likelihood to give in to crisis urges, make those things less accessible. For example, if you are targeting self-harm urges, either get rid of or make it difficult to access implements you might use for self-harm. If seeing certain things on social media triggers you, limit your access to social media.

Set up a challenge. Give yourself a skills challenge. Challenge yourself to use ten skills a day. Provide rewards to yourself for accomplishing this challenge.

Find an accountability partner. Pairing with someone to learn and motivate each other's skills use can be very effective. If you don't know anyone who might be interested in working on these skills, look for support groups in your area.

Be nice to yourself. Change is hard. Even small changes can be celebrated. Every step you take forward is a step toward your goal. Progress is almost never linear. Look at your progress over time rather than deciding a single setback means you are back at step 1.

Staying Focused on Your Goals

As you are pursuing your goals, you might find your emotion mind showing up. Sometimes, you might think that you don't have to focus on a certain problem behavior because you feel sure you will never do it again. Check in with wise mind, which will likely tell you that behavior still needs to be focused on.

Remember, small steps. Give yourself the satisfaction of reaching smaller goals along the way to larger goals. I know someone who loves her to-do lists. But she loves her completed to-do lists even more. She calls them ta-done lists (a mix of ta-da and to-do) and hangs them up to remind herself of what she has accomplished. How can you remind yourself of your small successes?

After doing DBT for a while, you may feel like it isn't working for you. That may be true. Or it may not be. Remember, when we are prone to emotional sensitivity our mood can sometimes convince us that our efforts are not making a difference when indeed they are.

Reaching out to some of the resources listed in the Resources section (page 158) can help when you start to doubt your progress. Hearing tales from others, and their struggles with maintaining their commitment and motivation, can be so validating and inspiring! Also, taking a look at your diary cards over time can help you appreciate the progress you have made. And, of course, finding a well-trained DBT therapist can help you move forward if you find yourself stuck.

If you find yourself, after you have checked all of the facts and worked those skills with all of your might, convinced that you are not moving forward, you may decide that DBT is truly not for you. In chapter 1 (page 3), I noted that there are other promising forms of treatment for BPD. Checking those out may help you find your path to success.

Tips for Staying Motivated

Although it's natural that your motivation level will wax and wane over time, these tips will help you stay on track in the long run.

Keep long-term goals in mind. Always return to that goal of living a life worth living. Keep in touch with wise mind regularly to stay on track. Keep a visual or physical reminder of your larger goals. Talk to people you respect about your goals and check in with them. Refine your goals from time to time (but never when in emotion mind). To make your larger goals more real in your day-to-day life, take note of the small progress you make toward them.

Use your experiences as learning opportunities. When times get tough, it can be hard to see the upside. One way to look at setbacks and challenges is to see them as opportunities to build mastery by using skills. Another way is proving to yourself that you can do hard things and still manage. Although these experiences will still be difficult, viewing them also as learning opportunities can at least make them more meaningful.

Practice patience. Emotion regulation involves slowing down and getting better at feeling the emotions we don't want to feel in order to discover that they aren't so horrible after all. It isn't that they aren't unpleasant, as they certainly are. However, difficult emotions can be overcome. Any practice we can get in building patience can only help with that. It takes time to achieve your goals. Quitting is fast, but then you don't achieve your goals. So, practice patience. Progress may be slower than you like. But at least you are on your way!

KEY TAKEAWAYS

You've come a long way through this workbook! Please give yourself major props for your efforts! Our final chapter together has been all about staying focused and motivated to achieve your goals. You've learned about using the diary card. You've seen the power of chain and solution analysis. As you move forward, it will be helpful to keep in mind:

- Chain analysis and solution analysis are incredibly helpful in understanding and solving the factors that lead to behaviors that get in the way of your life worth living.

- Daily use of the diary card gives you time to mindfully reflect on your day, keeps skill use top of mind, and helps track your progress.

- Doing skills plans for problematic behaviors before you engage in them gives you a road map to the skillful behavior you want to achieve.

- Remember to encourage and praise yourself in your efforts. Being skillful isn't always easy. Celebrate every step forward.

- Remember, you can return to this book at any time when you need a refresher.

A Final Note

Dear reader, thanks for joining me here. BPD can be a hard road, and I applaud you for taking steps to reduce your suffering. BPD is not a life sentence. Research studies following people with BPD indicate that life can and does get better for them. Please hold on to that when times get tough and your motivation to be skillful wanes. I hope you keep this book at hand as you continue your journey. The skills covered here have been helpful to many as an aid in their recovery from BPD.

Practicing skills on a regular basis is important to recovery. The more you use skills, especially when every cell in your body is screaming at you to give in to crisis urges and destructive behaviors, the more these new ways of managing your life and emotions will become a natural part of your behavioral repertoire. The more you use skills, the easier and more natural they will become. The best way to learn DBT is by putting it into practice. I urge you to put these skills to work over and over again.

I've listed lots of resources that can assist you on your path to being more effective in managing emotions. I want to wish you all the luck and courage in the world in your journey toward emotion regulation, overcoming BPD, and creating your life worth living. I truly hope this book has been helpful to you.

All my best to you,

–Suzette

Resources

APPS

Calm is a mindfulness app featuring hundreds of calming practices.

DBT Coach is an app that allows you to practice and track DBT skills used.

DBT Diary Card & Skills Coach is an app with a DBT reference section as well as a fillable diary card you can send to your therapist.

Headspace has a range of meditations and mindfulness practices.

BOOKS

Borderline Personality Disorder Journal: DBT Prompts and Practices to Manage Symptoms and Achieve Balance by Whitney Frost

The Borderline Personality Disorder Survival Guide: Everything You Need to Know About Living with BPD by Alexander L. Chapman and Kim L. Gratz

Building a Life Worth Living by Marsha M. Linehan

The High-Conflict Couple: A Dialectical Behavior Therapy Guide to Finding Peace, Intimacy, and Validation by Alan E. Fruzzetti

Loving Someone with Borderline Personality Disorder by Shari Y. Manning

Mindfulness for Borderline Personality Disorder: Relieve Your Suffering Using the Core Skill of Dialectical Behavior Therapy by Blaise Aguirre and Gillian Galen

The Mindfulness Solution for Intense Emotions: Take Control of Borderline Personality Disorder with DBT by Cedar R. Koons

The Miracle of Mindfulness by Thich Nhat Hanh

FINDING CERTIFIED DBT PROVIDERS

The Behavioral Tech website contains a listing of clinicians who are certified in DBT by the DBT-Linehan Board of Certification (DBT-LBC). Find it at BehavioralTech.org/resources/find-a-therapist.

HELP DURING A CRISIS

Call 988 (toll-free) for the **Suicide and Crisis Lifeline**

Text HELLO to 741-741 for free, twenty-four-hour support from the **Crisis Text Line**

Outside the United States, visit the **International Association for Suicide Prevention** (iasp.info) for a database of resources

WEBSITES

BorderlinePersonalityDisorder.org/family-connections
This is the website for the National Education Alliance for Borderline Personality Disorder's Family Connections™ Program, a twelve-week evidence-based program for loved ones of folks who struggle with emotional dysregulation. The website in general is a treasure trove of information about BPD.

DBTselfhelp.com
A website created by DBT users. It includes many helpful resources, including flash cards and diary cards that you can download and use.

HopeForBPD.com/my-dialectical-life-dbt-selfhelp
A subscription service for an emailed DBT skill of the day.

EmotionsMatterBPD.org
Emotions Matter is an organization created by a network of families and individuals affected by borderline personality disorder (BPD). Among many other resources, they offer a BPD peer-to-peer online support group.

References

American Psychiatric Association, *Diagnostic and Statistical Manual of Mental Disorders*, 5th Edition. Washington, DC: American Psychiatric Association, 2013.

Chapman, Alexander L., and Kim L. Gratz. *The Borderline Personality Disorder Survival Guide*. Oakland, CA: New Harbinger Publications, Inc., 2007.

"Core Evidence and Research." Behavioral Tech. BehavioralTech.org/research /evidence.

Corpstein, Liz. *DBT Workbook for Anxiety: Dialectical Behavior Therapy Strategies for Managing Worry, Stress, and Fear*. Oakland, CA: Rockridge Press, 2022.

"For What Conditions Is DBT Effective?" Behavioral Tech. BehavioralTech.org /research/evidence/for-what-conditions-is-dbt-effective-2.

Fruzzetti, Alan E. *The High-Conflict Couple: A Dialectical Behavior Therapy Guide to Finding Peace, Intimacy, and Validation*. Oakland, CA: New Harbinger Publications, Inc., 2006.

Harned, Melanie S., Safia C. Jackson, Katherine A. Comtois, and Marsha M. Linehan. "Dialectical Behavior Therapy as a Precursor to PTSD Treatment for Suicidal and/or Self-Injuring Women with Borderline Personality Disorder." *Journal of Traumatic Stress* 23, no. 4 (2010): 421–29. doi:10.1002 /jts.20553.

Linehan, Marsha M. *Building a Life Worth Living: A Memoir*. New York: Random House, 2020.

Linehan, Marsha M. *Cognitive-Behavioral Treatment of Borderline Personality Disorder*. New York: The Guilford Press, 1993.

Linehan, Marsha M. *DBT Skills Training Handouts and Worksheets*, 2nd edition. New York: The Guilford Press, 2015.

Linehan, Marsha M. *DBT Skills Training Manual*, 2nd edition. New York: The Guilford Press, 2015.

Porr, Valerie. *Overcoming Borderline Personality Disorder: A Family Guide for Healing and Change*. New York: Oxford University Press, 2010.

Rizvi, Shireen L. *Chain Analysis in Dialectical Behavior Therapy*. New York: The Guilford Press, 2019.

Stanley, Barbara and Gregory K. Brown. "Safety Plan Treatment Manual to Reduce Suicide Risk: Veteran Version." sefbhn.org/assets/zero-suicide -recommended-evaluation-tools/safety-plans/stanley-brown-safety -manual.pdf (accessed October 12, 2022).

Stiglmayr, Christian, Julia Stecher-Mohr, Till Wagner, Jeannette Meissner, Doreen Spretz, Christiane Steffens, Stefan Roepke, et al. "Effectiveness of Dialectic Behavioral Therapy in Routine Outpatient Care: The Berlin Borderline Study." *Borderline Personality Disorder and Emotion Dysregulation* 1, no. 1 (September 2015): 20. doi:10.1186/2051-6673-1-20.

Index

Acknowledgments

As always, thanks to my son Finn for his willingness to let his mom spend time at the computer instead of with him. You are the light of my life, and there is a mom and son road trip in your future, boy! Love and gratitude to my brother, Tom, for Sunday dinners and emotional support. Best Brother Ever. Extra special thanks to my clinical team of Liz Corpstein, Yulia Fox, and Vanessa Campos for their commitment to providing high-quality DBT. And, of course, to all of my clients who have taught me so much about living with and overcoming BPD. You are inspiring.

About the Author

 Suzette Bray, LMFT, is a licensed marriage and family therapist based in Los Angeles, California. She is the founder of mental health treatment programs for individuals and families impacted by borderline personality disorder and is the author of *DBT Explained* and *Your Emotions and You*. Suzette is a sought-after speaker and trainer on topics related to emotional health. You can find out more about Suzette at suzettebray.com.